BREAKING THE LOGJAM:
Obstacles to Forest Policy Reform in Indonesia and the United States

Charles Victor Barber
Nels C. Johnson
Emmy Hafild

WORLD RESOURCES INSTITUTE

March 1994

Kathleen Courrier
Publications Director

Brooks Belford
Marketing Manager

Hyacinth Billings
Production Manager

Cover Photo by Daniel Dancer
This photo shows the dramatic boundary between a roadless natural forest area in Washington state's Gifford Pinchot National Forest on the left and the clearcut landscape owned by a large industrial forest corporation on the right.

Each World Resources Institute Report represents a timely, scholarly treatment of a subject of public concern. WRI takes responsibility for choosing the study topics and guaranteeing its authors and researchers freedom of inquiry. It also solicits and responds to the guidance of advisory panels and expert reviewers. Unless otherwise stated, however, all the interpretation and findings set forth in WRI publications are those of the authors.

Contents

Acknowledgments

This publication is the result of a long and winding trail of research and writing. We wish to thank the many who helped us along the way. In particular, Walt Reid, Bob Repetto, Kenton Miller, Tom Fox, and Nigel Sizer at WRI offered helpful research guidance and generously detailed comments on earlier drafts. Steve Lanou provided invaluable assistance with research, fact-checking, and graphics.

Outside of WRI, we benefitted from reviews by Suraya Afiff, Jim Britell, Jim Douglas, Brock Evans, Abdon Jeff Olson, Al Sample, Roger Sedjo, and Professor Achmad Sumitro. In Indonesia, Suraya Afiff, Sandra Moniaga, Abdon Nababan, and Tri Nugroho provided key information. We also wish to thank the many other people, too numerous to mention here, in the U.S. Pacific Northwest and Indonesia who shared information and otherwise contributed to our research along the way. Emmy Hafild thanks the Institute of Environmental Studies at the University of Wisconsin/Madison for its support of her research.

Kathleen Courrier's editing made this publication much more concise and readable than it otherwise would have been. Thanks also go to Hyacinth Billings for coordinating production of the report. Finally, recognition goes to Donna Dwiggins and Ann Klofkorn for their efforts to help with revisions and otherwise get a long-delayed publication out the door.

The authors each wish to acknowledge the forbearance of their spouses during the research and writing of this publication.

C.V.B.
N.C.J.
E.H.

Foreword

Even cultures that long ago turned their forests into whatever seemed more immediately useful still celebrate the forest primeval in religions and myths passed down over millennia. From ancient Athens to the British empire, seagoing powers turned forests into sailing ships. During the Industrial Revolution, European countries used their forests—and their colonies' forests—to feed the growth of manufacturing and commerce. In its nineteenth-century push westward, the United States converted forests into farms and cities and railroad ties, even as Brazil is now fueling its steel industry with rainforest charcoal and Indonesia is exporting plywood to stoke its rapid economic growth.

Once let alone, damaged forests can recover as long as the assaults leveled at them haven't overwhelmed nature's regenerative powers. But in many parts of the world, forests are now under a virtual death sentence. At least 15 million hectares of tropical forest are vanishing each year, taking with them plant and animal species and indigenous peoples and leaving the world a poorer place, both biologically and culturally. In the temperate zones, forests are being fragmented by commercial logging, injured by pollution, converted to tree plantations or farmland, or falling victim to urban and suburban sprawl.

In *Breaking the Logjam: Obstacles to Forest Policy Reform in Indonesia and the United States*, Charles Barber and Nels Johnson of WRI and Emmy Hafild of Indonesia's Sejati Foundation examine the origins and impacts of current forest policies and recommend ways to make forest management more sustainable in two of the most important forested countries. The two countries differ in many ways, but both have forestry policies established in an earlier era and increasingly out of step with evolving perceptions of forests' true worth. As a result, many forests are under siege in both countries, and powerful forces are arrayed against the policy changes needed to maintain forests' health and productivity.

The authors of this report chose to focus on the United States and Indonesia to underscore the emerging scientific consensus that forests are in trouble *everywhere*—and the emerging political consensus that the North cannot deplore tropical deforestation while turning a blind eye to its own troubled woodlands. The authors demonstrate that overcoming the obstacles to more sustainable forest management in both countries will require grappling with three sets of issues: forest property rights regimes, the distribution of the costs and benefits of forest exploitation, and the political process for determining forest policies. All forested countries can learn from the experience of these two, since all face similar problems.

Specifically, *Breaking the Logjam* spells out how these two particular countries could deal with property rights, forest economics, and the forest policy-making process. But at its heart is a more general point: preserving and using the world's forests wisely depends as much on how a nation's political economy and political process works as on whether new technologies are adopted or particular forest-sector policies reformed.

Indeed, the report argues that in both Indonesia and the United States, the technical and policy changes needed to sustain forests are already well-known. Neither national government lacks knowledge, but the political will to remake their forest policies in the face of fierce opposition from powerful entrenched interests that benefit from current arrangements is missing. In this context, the authors maintain, forest policy reform must be broadened to encompass the structural elements of national economies, legal systems, and policy-making processes.

Breaking the Logjam extends the analyses and policy recommendations put forth in such WRI studies as *Surviving the Cut: Natural Forest Management in the Humid Tropics* and *The Forest for the Trees: Government Policies and the Misuse of Forest Resources*. To carry the work forward, WRI researchers are now beginning regional and local research on issues of sustainable forest management policy in East Africa, Amazonia, Mexico, mainland Southeast Asia, and New Guinea. In the United States, WRI is looking at the role of forests in a sustainable society under the aegis of its new "U.S. Sustainability Project."

We would like to express our appreciation to the Dutch Ministry of Foreign Affairs, the Norwegian Royal Ministry of Foreign Affairs, the Swedish International Development Authority, the United Nations Development Programme, the Canadian International Development Agency, The Surdna Foundation, the Sasakawa Peace Foundation, and the W. Alton Jones Foundation for their generous support of WRI's general research on forest and biodiversity conservation issues. For their foresight and support, we are deeply grateful.

Jonathan Lash
President
World Resources Institute

I. Introduction

When *Foreign Affairs* published an article on tropical deforestation in 1984 (Guppy, 1984), more than a few eyebrows were raised. What, many readers wondered, do forests have to do with diplomacy and national security? Eight years later, more than 100 Heads of State and Government and some 30,000 other participants in the "Earth Summit" and related meetings in Brazil took it as a matter of course that the fate of the forests—both temperate and tropical—deserved the international attention it was beginning to get. In a political twinkling, the contentious issue of accelerating forest destruction in the tropics had government agencies, the mass media, corporations, and a growing number of environmental organizations in its grip.

Tropical forests have become a political issue for a number of reasons. They contain 50 to 90 percent of the planet's species diversity. (Reid and Miller, 1989) They are home to many millions of the world's indigenous, tribal, and other traditional peoples who depend on them for livelihood—and in some cases, cultural survival. (Durning, 1992; Myers, 1989) And in gross area, tropical forests are shrinking far faster than temperate forests. (Dudley, 1992; WRI, 1992)

The fate of temperate and boreal forests like those in the U.S. Pacific Northwest has aroused concern for somewhat different reasons. Roughly half of the world's forests lie in temperate regions, nearly one quarter in the former USSR alone and nearly one fifth in North America. (UN-ECE/FAO, 1992) While total temperate forest area

grew between 1980 and 1990 (WRI, 1992), threats from airborne pollutants, the loss of biodiversity (as diverse natural forests give way to monocultural tree farms), and the conversion of forest lands to other uses are growing. In 1988, an estimated 40 percent of Europe's forests showed signs of damage from ozone, sulfur dioxide, and other gasses emitted in various economic activities. (Bundestag, 1990) A 1990 International Institute for Applied Systems Analysis (IIASA) study concluded that in 75 percent of Europe's forests sulfur deposition has reached damaging levels, at a cost of some $30 billion annually.[1] (IIASA, 1990)

In the United States, primary forests have been reduced to mere islands compared to their original expanse. Decades of intensive forest management and fire-fighting in the western United States have transformed forest ecosystems and increased the risk of catastrophic fires and the outbreak of introduced pathogens. (Norse, 1990; Perry, 1988; Showalter and Means, 1988; Agee and Huff, 1987) In the mixed mesophytic forests of the Cumberland Plateau west of the Appalachians, mounting evidence testifies to spreading forest decline. (Little, 1991) Like the losses documented at high elevations in the Appalachians (Bruck, 1989; Johnson and Siccama, 1989), these signs of stress may stem from decades of pollution that acidifies the soil, damages root systems, and makes trees more vulnerable to diseases and pests. In Canada, where far more trees are logged than planted, some 200,000 hectares are now lost each year. (Postel and Ryan, 1993) And eastern Russia's relatively unexploited forests appear to be on the brink of a massive logging boom. (Dudley, 1992; Levin, 1992)

Official responses to worsening forest conditions in the past decade include international efforts—such as the creation of the Tropical Forestry Action Plan (TFAP) and the International Tropical Timber Organization (ITTO)—and an explosion of national action plans, strategies, programs, and projects. Still, the health of the world's forests continues to wane, and narrow management approaches based on forestry cannot make headway against the economic, political, and social forces that largely determine the forests' future.

Taking a broader view of the forest crisis and understanding the key structural obstacles to making forest management and use more sustainable in the 21st century requires wrestling with three sets of issues: forest property rights regimes, the distribution of the costs and benefits of forest management and use, and the political process for determining forest policies. In this report, the cases of Indonesia and the United States are analyzed to reflect the emerging scientific consensus that forests in *all* parts of the world are more or less in trouble and the emerging political consensus that the North can no longer point a finger at the declining forests of the tropics without also looking to its own threatened backyards, and that protecting the global climate system will require southern countries to take an interest in northern forests. Considering these two important forest countries together also makes it clear that all nations with forests face some of the same problems.

Of course, Indonesia and the United States are not in exactly the same boat. Per capita Gross National Product (GNP) is $21,000 in the United States and $490 in Indonesia (WRI, 1992), and in general these two countries' historical, cultural, ecological, political, and economic profiles differ greatly. Certainly, the forest policies and practices of one country should not be embraced wholesale by the other, and little is to be gained by trying to decide which has the best forest policies. On the other hand, the countries may have

more in common than is usually supposed. Compare, for instance, the rapid clearing of forests in Indonesia over the past several decades of robust economic growth with what happened in the United States in the 19th and early 20th centuries. In any case, the issues addressed in *Breaking the Logjam* lie at the root of the forest challenges facing each country.

The international dimensions of the forest crisis in these two countries, such as trade or international agreements are not discussed here. Since the clear message of the United Nations Conference on Environment and Development (UNCED) from all governments was that forests are a sovereign *national* resource, the onus is now on governments and their citizens to take stock of local and national social and economic pressures on this resource. Indeed, these are some of the most fundamental forces harming forests, and little or no international agreement or assistance is required to defuse them. Property rights regimes, for example, have enormous impacts on forests, and efforts to put forest management on a more sustainable footing are unlikely to be effective if these and other such "structural" forces aren't understood and reconfigured.

Elements of Sustainable Forest Management

The basic arguments put forth in this report are that forests are under siege in both Indonesia and the United States, that forest policies in both countries need to be changed, and that powerful obstacles outside the forestry sector will make that change extremely difficult. But a positive vision of what good forest management would look like in any country underlies the analysis. That vision rests on four pillars:

1. *Ecological Integrity and Sustainability*: The country's forest estate contains effectively protected representative samples of all major forest types in areas large and connected enough to support the many environmental functions and services that forests provide—among them, the maintenance of forest-based biological diversity;

the protection of watersheds and the preservation of other aspects of hydrological systems; the maintenance of key nutrient-recycling functions; the protection of local climates and microclimates; and the sequestration and storage of carbon.

2. Sustainable and Equitable Human Uses of Forest Products and Services: Parts of the forest estate are strictly protected or utilized only for scientific research, limited traditional harvesting of flora and fauna, or low-impact nature tourism. Other areas are kept in permanent forest cover, but produce diverse economic goods and services, ranging from timber and other forest products to nature tourism benefits and genetic resources for agricultural, pharmaceutical, and biotechnology industrial activity—without compromising ecological services. Exactly how forest lands get used depends on an inventory of ecological characteristics, social and demographic factors, and economic potential. The economic costs and benefits of both forest conservation and production are equitably shared among local communities, the private sector, and the government.

3. Integrated Management at the Right Scale: Forests are managed within a regional framework of planning, decision-making, and management that takes into account surrounding human settlements, agricultural lands, and diverse economic activities. Ecological and social considerations determine the size of the management region. It is large enough to maintain the integrity of the region's ecological processes and to encompass the communities that understand, manage, and use the forest and related resources. But it is small enough for its people to call it home. Within this framework, governmental, community, corporate, and other interests together define development options for meeting human needs sustainably for both public and private land and decide land-use issues. (Foresters and a "forestry sector" still play a key role, but they are part of a team, not isolated specialists with a monopoly on decisions about the forest.)

4. Equitable and Informed Participation by all Stakeholders: In forest policy and management decisions—whether at regional or other levels—all stakeholders have the capacity and the right to information and participation. Decisions are made through an ongoing dialogue. Full information about the issues at hand gets to all participants in a timely manner and in forms all can understand. The inherent inequality of access to information and bargaining strength among participants—large corporations compared to local farmers, for example—is acknowledged, and government and intermediary non-governmental organizations work to strengthen the capacity of weak and marginalized groups to defend their own interests. The special situations and long-term claims of indigenous, traditional forest-dwelling, or forest-dependent communities are considered explicitly in law and in decision-making.

Is management that reflects these four goals a utopian dream? However difficult, moving forest management in this direction is not unrealistic. Indeed, a wide range of analysts have recently advocated similar goals (e.g., Cleaver et al., 1992; Dudley, 1992; Ramakrishna and Woodwell, 1992; Sharma, 1992; Aplet et al., 1993; Johnson and Cabarle, 1993). Their shared conclusion is that *not* taking steps toward more sustainable and equitable forest management is unrealistic. A recent comprehensive review organized by the World Bank concluded that "destructive exploitation of forests has caused serious economic, social, and environmental losses." (Sharma 1992) A 1992 United Nations review noted that the costs of watershed deforestation in the Asia-Pacific region reach many millions of dollars and that "urgent action is needed to develop preventive and remedial measures" to deal with the growing tracts of critically degraded forest lands. (ESCAP 1992) Dozens of similar reports on all parts of the world could be cited as well. While the exact formulation of what sustainable and equitable forest management would look like will vary somewhat by proponent and place—certainly the one put forth here is neither novel nor unique—the time is past when policy-makers and citizens need to ask *whether* change is needed.

In this report, we make the case for the types of changes needed in two countries, and examine the structural obstacles that stand in the way.

3

Indonesia's Forests: Context, Conditions, and Trends

With 185 million citizens, Indonesia is the world's fourth most populous country and one of the most culturally diverse. Emerging as an independent nation in 1945 after centuries under colonial rule, Indonesia has developed rapidly over the past several decades and boasts numerous economic and social successes. Among other achievements, it has boosted agricultural production, developed industry, lessened poverty, upgraded health care and education, and developed impressive transportation and communications networks. While Indonesia numbered among the poorest countries in the world in 1967, with a per capita GNP of only $50, and by 1970 some 60 percent of the population lived in absolute poverty, by 1987, that figure had dropped to 17 percent, despite an overall population increase and international economic stagnation from 1983 to 1987. (World Bank 1990)

Much of this growth and development has been fueled by the exploitation of Indonesia's rich natural resources, primarily petroleum but also timber, minerals, and agricultural commodities. Until the late 1970s, attention to the environmental impacts of resource exploitation was scant, but since then both government and non-governmental organizations have tried to strike a balance between economic growth and environmental sustainability. So far, the long-term health, diversity, and productivity of the nation's forests have not been ensured, but this judgment must be put in context:

- Virtually every country on earth has fueled its economic and social development by exploiting its natural resources at some point in its history.

- Unlike many developing countries, Indonesia has not squandered all its patrimony: a good share of the proceeds of natural resources exploitation have been plowed back into economic and social development.

- While environmental degradation and associated human problems still take a terrible

toll in Indonesia—and are in some cases growing worse—the government at the highest levels is taking these problems seriously and has in the past decade begun to address them head on.

For Indonesia, geography has been destiny. The country comprises more than 13,000 islands that span the equator and stretch upwards of 5,000 km from east to west. These far-flung islands are home to the world's second largest expanse of tropical rain forest, covering about 109 million hectares or 56 percent of the land area. (GOI/FAO, 1990) Of the 19 distinct forest types identified so far, (Dick, 1991), lowland evergreen forest predominates, accounting for some 55 percent of the total in the Outer Islands.[2] Borneo alone boasts an estimated 1,800 to 2,300 tree species larger than 10 cm in diameter, and some 40 plant genera and many more species are endemic to this lush island. Of the 650 bird species known or presumed to breed on the Sunda shelf (which includes Peninsular Malaysia, Sumatra, Borneo and Java), 291 inhabit inland lowland forests. (Wells, 1971) *Dipterocarpaceae*, with some 386 species in western Indonesia, dominate these forests and yield the most commercial hardwood. Peat swamp forests blanket stretches of Sumatra and some parts of Kalimantan, while smaller areas of sub-montane and montane forests are scattered throughout the country. Heathlike forests in sandy soils dot Kalimantan, while Australian flora occurs in some eastern parts of the country (RePPProT 1990).

While Indonesia occupies only 1.3 percent of the world's land area, it possesses up to 17 percent of the planet's species. Roughly and conservatively, Indonesia houses about 11 percent of the world's flowering plant species, 12 percent of the world's mammals, 17 percent of all birds, and at least 37 percent of the world's fish. (KLH, 1992) Much of this astounding diversity owes its existence to the country's extensive and diverse forests.

Some of the biologically richest in the world, Indonesian forests are also among the most exploited. While on paper 14 percent (16 million hectares) of remaining forest is protected in parks and reserves, many such areas are scarred by logging, mining, agriculture, and new human settlements *(See Figure 1.1.)*

Forest cover in 1950 (when the last comprehensive forest inventory was completed) was estimated at about 152 million hectares. (IIED/GOI, 1985) Data collected around 1985 suggest a current forest cover of 119 million hectares (RePPProT 1990) Thus, losses averaged 914,000 hectares annually for 35 years. Deforestation was especially intense during the second half of the period, when large-scale commercial timber extraction accelerated dramatically. When the 1985 and subsequent data were reinterpreted in 1991, analysts concluded effective forest cover in late 1989 totalled 109 million hectares and that the annual deforestation rate was then 1.3 million hectares. (GOI, 1991b) These remaining 109 million hectares contain substantial logged-over areas in varying states of degradation. (All of these figures are tentative, but are the best currently available.) *(See Figure 1.2.)*

Deforestation in Indonesia has five main causes:

- Forest clearing by growing numbers of migrant farmers who cultivate both subsistence and cash crops;

- Large-scale commercial logging operations;

- Conversion of natural forests to large-scale commercial agriculture and timber plantations;

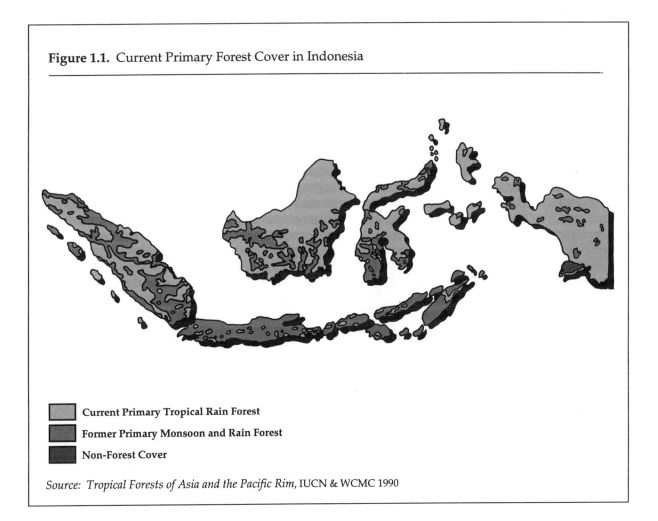

Figure 1.1. Current Primary Forest Cover in Indonesia

☐ **Current Primary Tropical Rain Forest**

☐ **Former Primary Monsoon and Rain Forest**

■ **Non-Forest Cover**

Source: Tropical Forests of Asia and the Pacific Rim, IUCN & WCMC 1990

5

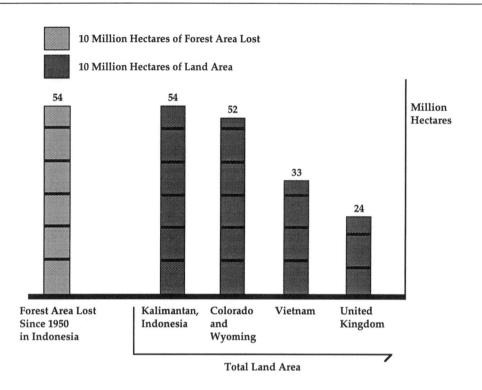

Figure 1.2. Area of Lost Forest Cover in Indonesia Compared to Selected Country Land Areas

Source: IIED/GOI 1985 and Rand McNally & Co., 1982. *The Great Geographical Atlas,* Rand McNally, Chicago.

- The government's official transmigration program, which resettles people from the crowded islands of Java and Bali onto cleared forest lands on the less densely populated islands of Kalimantan, Sumatra, Sulawesi, and Irian Jaya; and

- The expansion of mining, oil exploration and production, and other forms of industrial development into forested areas.

These factors interact synergistically. Logging, mining, and transmigration open forest lands to cultivators and spontaneous settlement. As the forest is degraded, it becomes a target for conversion to timber plantations or perennial crops. These activities in turn attract more migrants, even though the agricultural potential of much cleared land drops rapidly. The aggregate effect is to slow or stop the forest's regrowth. *(See Figure 1.3.)*

Although Indonesia's government is beefing up reforestation programs (GOI, 1991a), the emphasis is on fast-growing softwood species grown on monocultural tree farms. Unfortunately, such plantations do little to reduce pressure on tropical moist forests (World Bank 1991b), and for local communities, tree farms do not provide the income and products the natural forests do. (Friends of the Earth 1992; WALHI/LBH, 1992)

Indonesian law places control and management of all forest lands in the hands of the Ministry of Forestry and its regional offices. *(See*

Figure 1.3. Sources and Evolution of Deforestation in Indonesia
Relative size of arrow indicates magnitude of deforestation

Time →

Logging

Transmigration

Encroachment and
Traditional Agriculture

Forest Fires

Estate Crops

Swampland Development

Source: Dick, 1991

Chapter II.) A parallel structure of provincial forestry services operated by provincial governments supplies most technical services. Various donor organizations and multilateral development banks—most notably, the World Bank and the Asian Development Bank—fund forestry projects and programs and advise government on forest policy. Because the forest products industry is an important economic actor and comprises a relatively small number of firms, it too greatly influences forest policy. *(See Chapter III.)* In general, forest policy-making in Indonesia is a relatively insular, top-down process: other sectoral agencies of government outside the forestry department, provincial-level forestry officials, nongovernmental organizations, and the general public have a limited voice. *(See Chapter IV.)*

Policy studies carried out over the past decade, some commissioned by the Ministry of Forestry, have identified the key reforms needed to slow deforestation and make forest management more sustainable. The proposals include reforms of tenurial arrangements on forest lands (Moniaga, 1991; Zerner, 1990; Barber and Churchill, 1987), changes in the timber-concession system (WALHI, 1991; Gray and Hadi, 1989; Repetto et al., 1989; Boulter, 1988; Gillis, 1988); new forest-resource pricing (World Bank, 1989); the establishment of policies supporting forest-management partnerships with local communities (Poffenberger, 1990; Seymour and Rutherford, 1990); and the reconsideration of policies governing timber plantations (WALHI/LBH, 1992; ADB, 1992a; Nugroho, 1991; Sedjo, 1988) and shifting cultivation. (GOI/FAO, 1990; Weinstock, 1989) Acknowledging many points raised in these studies, current government policy statements call for a comprehensive effort to slow deforestation (IFAP, 1991), and they commit Indonesia to biodiversity conservation. (KLH, 1992; GOI, 1991b) In a February 1993 speech (Soeharto 1993), President Soeharto noted that:

> We, in Indonesia, are well aware of the importance of dealing with forest and forestry issues.... Forests play an important role in the climatic condition and sustain the soil and water. Furthermore, forests also serve as diverse biological resources and as a storehouse of genetic resources...We are aware of the host of things that still must be improved or perfected in putting into practice the principle of sustainable forest management. For this purpose, we will be pleased to receive criticism and recommendations as well as assistance from experts, countries and donor institutions in order to support sustainable forestry development and management, as mandated by the Earth Summit.

Yet, even with such high-level political commitment, change within an entrenched system of forest management and exploitation is slow. The current challenge is thus not so much determining what policy changes are needed as it is understanding and addressing the basic structural issues that both fuel forest degradation and loss in Indonesia and frustrate reform.

U.S. Forests: Context, Conditions and Trends

The United States, with nearly 300 million hectares of forest and woodland, is one of the world's most extensively forested countries, trailing only Russia, Brazil, and Canada. (WRI, 1992) Although less biologically diverse than Indonesia's forests, American woodlands include temperate, boreal, and tropical forest types. *(See Table 1.1.)* Forests are most extensive in the eastern half of the country, where deciduous hardwood forests stretch along the east coast from the Florida peninsula to northern New England and west to the Mississippi River, except where agriculture (especially in the Midwest) and urban areas (especially along the east coast) have replaced natural ecosystems. West of the Mississippi, beyond the broad sweep of the Great Plains, predominantly coniferous forests are found in the mountains rising above the semi-arid grasslands and deserts. Along the Pacific coast from central California to southeastern Alaska lie the world's most diverse coniferous forests. *(See Box 1.1.)* They harbor trees unequalled anywhere for size, height, and age. Vast boreal forests cover interior Alaska, while small patches of remnant humid tropical and dry tropical forest are found in Hawaii and Puerto Rico.

Before European settlers arrived, forests covered approximately 48 percent of what eventually became the United States. (Postel and Ryan, 1991) Today, forests cover about 32 percent of all U.S. land. (WRI, 1992) Many of these forests have at one time or another been heavily modified or cleared for agriculture. Although precise figures are not available, most estimates indicate that primary forests in the United States outside of Alaska have been reduced to less than 5 percent of their original extent[3]—a much smaller percentage than in Indonesia and most other tropical countries. (Postel and Ryan, 1991) *(See Figure 1.4.)* Still, the forest area in the United States has rebounded from all-time lows in the early 1900s, and—especially along the east coast—many lands once cleared for agriculture have reverted to forest. The country is now the world's largest producer and consumer of wood products and exporter of raw logs. (FAO, 1992)

Table 1.1. Selected Forest Statistics for Indonesia and the U.S.

	Indonesia	United States
Total Forest Area	109,000,000 HA[1]	226,450,000 HA[2]
Forest as Percent of Total Land Area	56[1]	32[2]
Percent of Original Primary Forest Remaining	43[3]	5[3,5]
Deforestation Rate (1980–90)	1.0[7]	0.1[4]
Production of Industrial Roundwood, 1988 (mil. m^3)	40[6]	417[6]
Share of Total World Production of Roundwood	2%[6]	25%[6]

1. From GOI/FAO, 1990
2. From WRI, 1992
3. From Postel and Ryan, 1991
4. From UN-ECE/FAO, 1993
5. Excluding Alaska
6. From UN FAO, "Forest Products Yearbook 1988"
7. From UN FAO, 1993, "Forest Resources Assessment 1990: Tropical Countries."

Despite this impressive comeback, many U.S. forests face cumulative and growing threats from pollution, urbanization, and unsustainable or inappropriate exploitation:

- Air pollution from automobiles and industrial sources kill and injure trees; they also leave trees more vulnerable to insects and disease;

- Large-scale commercial logging operations isolate biologically complex natural forests in ever smaller patches surrounded by younger increasingly simplified forest stands;

- The conversion of diverse natural forests to tree plantations leads to biological impoverishment, especially in the South and the Pacific Northwest;

- Introduced exotic pests and diseases (e.g., Gypsy moth, Chestnut blight, and Dutch elm disease) threaten native species and ecological relationships;

- Urban and suburban development displaces secondary forests on the fringes of most metropolitan areas; and

- The development of vacation homes, recreational facilities, mining, oil drilling, and road construction fragments and diminishes forests in rural areas.

Although these factors are chipping away at forest cover,[4] their principal effect is to narrow the range of forest products and services. For example, water quality and fisheries production have been seriously damaged by intensive logging and road-building in U.S. forest areas. (Anderson and Gerhke, 1988) From sugar maples and red spruce in northern New England to ponderosa pines in southern California, evidence of tree injury, mortality, and decreased growth in some areas has been at least partially attributed to pollution. (Bruck, 1989; Johnson and Siccama, 1989; Miller, 1989; MacKenzie and El-Ashry, 1989) Moreover, the lengthening list of species threatened and endangered as their habitats disappear indicates serious forest management problems.[5]

Unlike in Indonesia, in the United States, legal and management authority over forests is largely decentralized. Just under two thirds of the country's forests are owned by corporations or individuals. (USDA, 1989) Small individual land

Box 1.1. Old-Growth Forests in the United States Pacific Northwest

The battle over what remains of the Northwest's old-growth or "ancient forests" is one of America's most emotional political issues. Old-growth forests—defined in varying ways—are more than 250 years old. They contain large trees, big fallen logs, and large standing snags (dead trees). With a mixed and multi-layered canopy broken by occasional light-filled gaps, trees may grow up to 100 meters high and over 2 meters in diameter.

Since 1976, the National Forest Management Act has required the U.S. Forest Service to maintain viable populations of all vertebrate species throughout their range. Although the northern spotted owl (*Strix occidentalis caurina*) may be the most notorious resident of old growth forests, new research indicates these forests are the preferred, and sometimes only, habitat for a growing list of species (Booth, 1989), and mounting scientific evidence indicates that continued logging in old-growth forests will further endanger species. (e.g., Thomas, et. al, 1993)

We do not know exactly how extensive old-growth forests were before Euro-Americans arrived on the scene, but a reasonable estimate is that between 6 and 7.6 million hectares blanketed unsettled Oregon and Washington. (Norse, 1990) How much remains and how fast it is disappearing are questions at the center of heated debate among the timber industry, the U.S. Forest Service, scientists, and environmental groups. Haynes (1986) and Greene (1988),

both USFS researchers, estimated total old-growth in the two states in the mid 1980s at 1.3 and 1.8 million hectares respectively. But more recent analyses have produced lower estimates.

Morrison (1988) examined six national forests and identified only 456,000 hectares of old-growth—substantially less than the 638,000 hectares estimated by Haynes (1986) and the 1,001,000 hectares estimated in draft USFS environmental impact assessments for the same national forests. Extending Morrison's analysis, Norse (1990) estimated that the total area of old-growth forest now amounts to slightly over 1 million hectares, or 13 percent of what once was. Of this, approximately 470,000 hectares is protected in national parks, wilderness areas, or research natural areas.

If Norse and Morrison are correct, unprotected old-growth in the Northwest would disappear within 30 to 40 years at recent logging rates (approximately 19,000 hectares/year). However, since so much of what remains is fragmented or otherwise compromised by proximity to roads and clearcuts, the ecologically viable old-growth forest area outside of protected areas could disappear far faster. According to Norse (1990), with logging rates and harvesting patterns similar to those of the 1980's, any old growth forest remaining outside of protected areas would come under the damaging influence of windthrow and radical microclimatic shifts within 20–25 years.

---

owners control two thirds of those private forest lands, though corporations own comparatively more than small individual landowners in the Pacific Northwest and the South. Of public "owners," the U.S. Forest Service ranks first with 76 million hectares in 156 National Forests, most of them in the western states.

Not surprisingly, this pattern of forest land ownership has given rise to a patchwork of legislative mandates, regulations, and management jurisdictions. Federally owned forest lands are managed in accordance with at least two dozen major Acts of Congress. State and private forest lands do not come under federal law except to

Figure 1.4. Primary Forest Cover in the United States, 1620-1989

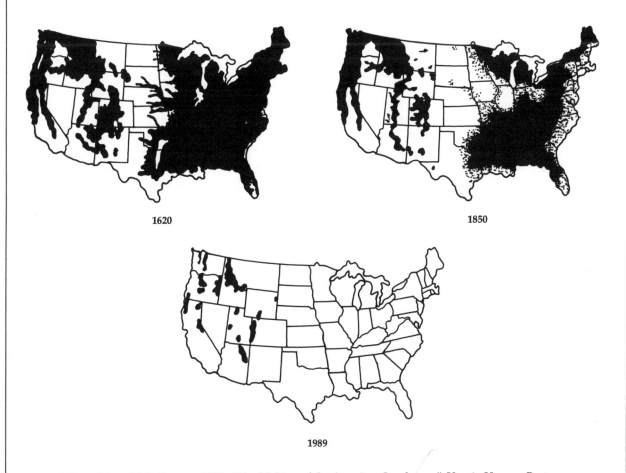

1620

1850

1989

Source: Adapted from M.P. Couzen, 1990. "The Making of the American Landscape", Unwin Hyman, Boston; and The Native Forest Council.

the extent that broad environmental statutes apply, such as the Endangered Species Act and the Clean Water Act. Some states have passed forest-practices acts that affect all or some of the non-federal forest lands, but most state forestry laws are limited in scope, and violations are usually treated as minor civil offenses or misdemeanors. Although some non-regulatory incentives to conserve forest resources do exist, their influence on forest management decisions by private land owners is not well understood.

A growing number of analysts have examined forest-management problems and proposed responses to them. Many studies that focus on the economics of below-cost sales of publicly-owned forest resources (e.g., Rice, 1989; O'Toole, 1988; Repetto, 1988) recommend ending timber sales where they cost more to administer than they generate in revenues, especially where environmental damage is likely. Studies of U.S. Forest Service conflicts with, evasion of, or negligence in carrying out environmental legislation,

11

especially the Endangered Species Act and the National Environmental Protection Act (e.g., Gordon et al., 1991; Norse, 1990; Thomas et al., 1990; Anderson and Gerkhe, 1988; Wilcove, 1988), recommend various reforms to protect forest resources other than timber. In general, the consensus is that the country's forest policies no longer suit the problems facing America's forests. (Aplet et al., 1993)

In response to this growing consensus, recent policy statements by the U.S. Forest Service and the Bureau of Land Management commit the federal government to ecosystem-management policies intended to prevent the environmental damage caused by intensive commodity-oriented forest management. (e.g., Robertson, 1992) Several states have recently passed laws to better protect forest resources on state and private lands, others are considering following suit, and some are working to develop innovative incentive programs to encourage more sustainable forest management. But the complex web of ownership, law, and perverse economic incentives that govern the use and management of U.S. forest lands impedes change. To break the policy logjam, advocates of more sustainable approaches to forest management will have to recognize and address basic structural issues—tenure, economics, and policy-making itself.

Notes

1. The actual breakdown is calculated by IIASA (1990) as the loss of unprocessed wood ($6.3 billion); loss of value-added processing in wood industry ($7.2 billion); and other costs including flood, erosion, and siltation damage ($16.2 billion).

2. Indonesian islands are customarily categorized as either fertile, intensively populated and cultivated "Inner Islands" (Java and Bali) or the mostly-forested, thinly populated "Outer Islands" (Sumatra, Kalimantan [Borneo], Sulawesi, and Irian Jaya are the largest).

3. Postel and Ryan (1991) indicate there are about 65 million hectares of primary forest in the United States, or 15 percent of all forest cover. However, most of it is in Alaska (52 million hectares), with only 13 million hectares remaining elsewhere. Most of the 13 million hectares is high-elevation alpine and sub-alpine forests in the western states, which typically have limited species diversity. Lower elevation primary forests are extremely rare. Noss (1990) estimates the total primary forest left in the Pacific Northwest (i.e., Douglas fir/western hemlock forests below approximately 1,250 meters) comprises about 1.0 million hectares. Primary forest area in the eastern United States (east of the Mississippi River) has been reduced to no more than between 100,000–200,000 hectares. (NEEN, 1992)

4. Between 1980 and 1990, the United Nations (UN-ECE/FAO, 1992) estimates that the United States lost 3.2 million hectares of forest—an average deforestation rate of 0.1 percent compared to Indonesia's 0.8 percent.

5. More than 150 endangered species are found in the National Forest System alone, and at least 1,300 species found on National Forest lands are candidates for formal designation. (Norse et al., 1986)

II. Ownership, Access, and Control over Forest Lands

Patterns of forest ownership, access, and control—collectively termed "tenure" here—create powerful incentives for sapping or saving forests. At base, forest tenure is a bundle of rights to occupy, use, or benefit from forests and forest lands under a particular system of law and authority. In most systems, such rights are linked—at least formally—to corresponding duties, such as that of a logging concession-holder to replant. In many, they invite poor forest management, and in all they bring economic benefit and political influence.

Property rights are among the most difficult social and legal relationships to change. To even raise the issue in the context of forestry is to stir up tensions over state versus community control of land and resources in Indonesia, and cries of unconstitutionality in the United States. Yet, policy-makers and others have no choice but to systematically bring tenurial issues into the debate over the forest's future if there is to be progress toward better policies.

Forest Tenure in Indonesia

In 1990, a consultant on forestry law opened a draft report for the Indonesian Ministry of Forestry on "Legal Options for the Indonesian Forestry Sector" (Zerner, 1990) by saying "The forests of Indonesia are an immense commons." The final version read: "The Government of Indonesia exercises complete jurisdiction and authority over designated forest lands totalling approximately 140 million hectares." This editorial change illustrates the fundamental tensions that underlie forest tenure and the obstacles that current perceptions and policies governing forest ownership, access, and control present to forest-policy reform. The government *does*, in fact, claim sole legal jurisdiction and authority over roughly 143 million hectares of designated forest land, some 74 percent of the country's land area. But these forest lands are also a vast "commons" insofar as a wide range of actors—from large timber companies to migrant cultivators and small-scale gold-panners—have loosely restricted access to them.[1] Such "open access" (Bromley 1989) is a powerful incentive to deforest and degrade lands since none of these actors holds a secure right to forest lands that might serve as an incentive for careful, long-term management, and none possess the practical means to control or exclude others, especially in remote areas.

But access to Indonesia's forests is not equal. Some who stake claims, especially wealthy and technically sophisticated logging firms, receive the state's imprimatur—concessionary legal rights to exploit particular forest territories and resources. Others without a shot at these concessions either appeal to customary law, which is honored mainly in the breach, or defy the law in protest or desperation.

In national parks and other protected forests, open access is the *de facto* law of the land too. Protected areas are legally off limits for almost all occupations and resource uses but the forest-conservation agency lacks the wherewithal to police illegal logging, farming, or settlement within park boundaries. Many Indonesian protected areas have thus become magnets for clandestine timber extraction, slash-and-burn farming, and wildlife collection.

This tenurial system gives rise to two problems. First, caught in a double bind, both commercial interests and communities are all but forced to degrade the forest, as they have done increasingly over the past several decades. Second, a major industry worth some $4 billion a year—logging and forest products—is founded on the basis of this forest-tenure system, and powerful firms and industry associations with a stake in this system exert tremendous influence on forest policy. In recent years, the government has stepped up enforcement of concession-management regulations and explored ways to reconcile local communities' land and resource rights more equitably with logging and other large-scale development activities in forest areas. But since the timber and forest products industry is so important to the national economy, reformers in government move cautiously.

The National Tenure System for Forest Lands

Under Indonesia's Constitution, authority and responsibility for "Branches of production which are important for the State and which affect the lives of most people," belongs to the state. Government controls and manages the nation's forests under the provisions and implementing regulations of the Basic Forestry Law of 1967, which empowers the Ministry of Forestry to "determine and regulate legal relations between individuals or corporate bodies and forests, and deal with legal activities related to forests."

Under the Basic Forestry Law, certain lands are classified by Ministerial Decree as official "Forest Area," contingent on an inventory, survey, and boundary determination. Deforested lands may be included in a Forest Area if they are slated for reforestation. In turn, Forest Areas are sub-classified as Limited or Regular "Production

Forests;" "Protection Forests" set aside to protect watersheds or erosion-prone slopes; "Conservation Forests," including National Parks and Nature Reserves; and "Recreation Forests," including Hunting and Tourism Parks. In addition, some forest lands are classified as Forest Available for Conversion to non-forest uses, while a small remainder are "Unclassified Forests." Under the province-by-province Consensus Forest Land Use Planning process (TGHK) undertaken in the early 1980s, government-controlled Forest Area in each province is divided into these various categories and recorded on official maps. *(See Table 2.1.)*

Tenurial rights over forest lands are determined by these categories; and, on balance, few kinds of rights to forest lands are permitted. Customary (*adat*) community rights in effect in many areas are recognized by national law only to the extent that they do not conflict with officially authorized uses of the forest. (Zerner, 1990; Barber and Churchill, 1987) In effect, traditional rights hold only until the tide of officially sanctioned development reaches a particular region or resource.

The most important forest property right is the 20-year Right of Forest Exploitation (HPH), which is:

> A right to exploit the forest in a Designated Forest Area, through cutting of timber, regenerating and caring for the forest, and processing and marketing forest products, in accordance with a Forest Exploitation Workplan, in line with existing regulations, and on the basis of conservation and sustainable production.[2]

As of 1991, some 580 such HPH concessions covering about 60 million hectares—31 percent of the country's land area—averaged about 105,000 hectares each. (Pramono, 1991; RePPProT, 1990) HPHs are granted by the Ministry of Forestry to Indonesian private or state-chartered corporations, though in practice some are held by joint ventures with foreign firms. Applications and renewals are approved by the Ministry of Forestry,

Table 2.1. Indonesian Forest Classifications and Use (in million hectares)

TGHK Forest Categories	Primary Purpose	Permitted Timber Extraction	Source* Official TGHK	RePPProt Transferred	RePPProt Revised
Nature Reserve	Genetic Conservation	None	18.25	17.32	25.11
Protection	Watershed Protection	None	29.68	31.20	55.09
Limited Production	Timber Production & Erosion Prevention	Selection Felling Only	30.52	30.13	12.57
Normal Production	Natural Timber Production	Selection or Clear Felling as Determined by Forest Type	31.85	30.76	18.26
Conversion	Potentially Convertible to Non-Forest Uses	Clear Felling	30.54	36.70	66.05**
Unclassified			38.45	30.97	

* Official: areas as quoted on official TGHK maps
RePPProt Transferred: data are measurements of existing TGHK categories transferred to RePPProt map
RePPProt Revised: suggested revisions reflecting more accurate assessments of existing forest cover
** Conversion and unclassified
Sources: RePPProt, 1990 and Dick, 1991

with a recommendation from the provincial Governor. (Barber, 1990)

In 1990, the Ministry of Forestry began granting Industrial Timber Plantation Rights (HPHTI), which allow holders to plant and harvest plantation timber on "unproductive" areas of Permanent Production Forest, to private or state firms and to officially recognized cooperatives for a term of 35 years plus one growing cycle of the dominant species planted. Under current plans, some 4.4 million hectares of state forest lands will be developed under these new concessions by 1999. (GOI, 1991b)

While a plantation concession can cover as much as 300,000 hectares,[3] most firms currently plan to plant only 60 to 70,000 hectares of this area and to cut natural forests in the remainder of the concession in the initial years before the plantation matures. (World Bank, 1993) Access to this residual natural forest (and to the land it sits on, once cleared) is a large *de facto* subsidy, in addition to a formal monetary subsidy the concession-holder[4] receives.

Various other minor rights extended on Indonesia's forest lands include rattan (*Palmae*, subfamily *Calamoidae*) cultivation concessions,[5] rights to collect wild rattan,[6] and a concessionary right to exploit sago (*Metroxylon spp.*) and nipah (*Nypa fruticans*) forests.[7] By law, the only tenurial right that may be granted on Indonesia's 30 million hectares of Protection Forests, or on its 18 million hectares of National Parks, Nature Reserves, and Recreation Forests is that to collect wild rattan in the Protection Forests—a comparatively minor enterprise.

A Profile of Customary Forest-Tenure Systems

The forest-tenure regime mandated by national law is relatively recent. Up until the last few decades, most forest lands used or inhabited by people were governed by customary *adat* law and authority (Abdurrahman 1984; Sudiyat 1981). In many local forest communities, *adat* still reigns and its authority—flowing not from the state but from the communities themselves—is often locally viewed as more legitimate, more ecologically sound, and more just.

Conceptions of tenure under *adat* differ radically from the underlying assumptions of the state's system. Under *adat*,

- Land has socio-religious significance, and it is closely connected to the identity of the group. Matters concerning land cannot easily be separated from matters of kinship, authority and leadership, modes of subsistence, ritual, and the supernatural.

- In many areas, land and its resources support a broad array of seasonally staggered activities. Rotational and shifting cultivation (swidden), hunting, fishing, and the collection of forest products generally predominate over sedentary, intensive agriculture or the intensive exploitation of a few species for the market.

- Individual, heritable rights in land exist, but most individual "rights in land" are either rights of use subsidiary to a superior group right, or rights to particular resources, such as rubber or other trees, or to harvest a particular cultivated plot. Thus land tenure and resource tenure aren't necessarily the same thing, and one parcel of land is often encumbered with a variety of rights held by different persons and groups.

- Unworked lands are, for the most part, as encumbered by rights as individual garden plots. Land is rarely considered "empty."

- Rights in land and its resources are rarely recorded in maps or written records, with the exception of ownership marks placed on trees and other discrete, individually owned resources. Borders are determined on the basis of natural features, such as rivers, and by mutual understandings.

Generally, *adat* rights in the forest are of three types: Rights to specific trees, both tended and growing wild and to other forest resources (e.g. game and fish); rights to use land once or now used for long-fallow swidden cultivation; and communal "rights of disposal" over land considered the homeland and property of a particular group or community.

Compared to forest rights created under the Basic Forestry Law, *adat* rights are weak and insecure under national law. The Basic Forestry Law says only that "The enjoyment of *adat* rights, whether individual or communal, to exploit forest resources directly or indirectly… may not be allowed to disturb the attainment of the purposes of this Law." A 1970 implementing regulation[8] further elaborates (and weakens) *adat* rights in HPH concession areas:

(1) The rights of the *adat* community and its members to harvest forest products … shall be organized in such manner that they do not disturb forest production.

(2) Implementation of the above provision is [delegated to the Company] which is to accomplish it through consensus with the *adat* community, with supervision from the Forest Service.

(3) In the interests of public safety, *adat* rights to harvest forest products in a particular area shall be frozen while forest production activities are under way.

The new laws and regulations governing timber-plantation, rattan, sago, and nipah concessions are completely silent on *adat*, even though complex *adat* systems of rights and obligations throughout the Indonesian archipelago govern the ownership and harvesting of, for example, rattan and sago. (Ngo, 1991; de Beer and McDermott, 1989; Barber and Churchill, 1987; Peluso, 1986) The HPH logging concession precedent suggests that new rights pertaining to these species invalidate conflicting *adat* rights.

The Basic Agrarian Law of 1960 does recognize customary law as the basis for national land law (Moniaga, 1991; Abdurrahman, 1984; Sudiyat, 1981). But three factors have made this law largely irrelevant to tracts classified as Forest Area under the Basic Forestry Law of 1967. First, few rural communities understand national laws and legal procedures. Indeed, one study in a Central Kalimantan village, for example, found that 87 percent of the people had never even heard of the Basic Agrarian Law (Moniaga, 1991), and customary rights have rarely been registered under its provisions in rural forest areas.[9] Second, much like the Basic Forestry Law of 1967, the Agrarian Law notes that customary law "applies to the land, water and air *as long as it does not contradict national and State interests…*" (emphasis added.) Finally, in practice, government has interpreted the Forestry Law as one that prevails over the Basic Agrarian Law in legally designated Forest Areas.

The Impacts of Indonesia's Forest-Tenure System

Indonesia's current forest-tenure system is working against the health of the nation's forests and against prospects for their sustainable management. By overriding traditional rights, the relatively new system of nationally sanctioned rights and access rules has eroded local communities' incentives to manage the forest for the long term and engendered social conflict in many areas. At the same time, the sheer scale and, in some cases, remoteness of areas under timber concessions, has overwhelmed government's ability to collect reliable data, set boundaries, and police concession-holders in the field. Then too, even if they were enforced, existing obligations are simply too weak to ensure the forest's long-term viability.

Since the Basic Forestry Law and the Law on Foreign Investment passed in 1967, and the logging industry subsequently boomed, forest-dwelling and forest-dependent communities in Indonesia's Outer Islands have lost rights of access, ownership, and control to the state apparatus and to the large commercial firms that it licenses to exploit those resources. In all, the traditional *adat* tenurial rights of millions of forest-dwelling and forest-dependent people have been handed over to a relatively small number of commercial firms and state enterprises, or, for conservation purposes, to the Ministry of Forestry.

The extent to which timber concessions and conservation areas have displaced settled *adat* rights in forest lands and resources remains uncertain, however. Official maps and records don't document customary rights, and no one really knows how many people live on government-designated forest lands or earn their living from them, or how extensive their territorial claims are. Estimates of the number of people living in or next to state-designated forest lands range from 1.5 to 65 million, depending on which definition is used and which policy agenda is at stake. The extent of forest territory claimed, controlled, or managed by forest-dwelling peoples and communities has never been surveyed systematically. Neither have overlaps between the boundaries or areas under community management and those of legally designated forest areas.

When development activities begin in such a legally uncharted area, local communities can do little to hang on to their traditional rights. One study of central Sumatra's lowland forests found that some traditional landowners attempt to acquire land title certificates to legitimize their *adat* claims under national law. But, the study found:

> …for the large majority of local people, securing their rights through obtaining certificates is not a realistic option. They have but one possibility left: to force the traditional land tenure system to its bitter end, hoping that at least some kind of recognition will be given to them when the land is expropriated.

17

Thus, their strategy is to clear as much land as possible within previously uncleared forest before somebody else does so. "We know we are destroying our forests, but it is a race and whoever does not join it will lose" is the fear expressed by villagers as they move to new forest areas. (Ostergaard, 1993)

At the heart of the issue is a perceptual conflict over the strength and validity of *adat* rights in the face of a new government-sponsored tenure system:

> …[Relationships between timber concessions, local land-use practices, and the ecological state of the forest] are determined by the concession system because the legal right to forest resources has been transferred from the traditional communities to the concession-holders. The local use of large timbers to build boats, for example, is obstructed by the rights of the concession-holder. Thus arises use of the term "theft" of timber owned by the concession-holder by the local people. For the local people, however, of course the problem is seen differently, as the "theft" of the wood by the concession-holder. (Haeruman, 1992)[10]

An example of this clash of perceptions is the case of the P.T. You Lim Sari (YLS) timber concession in northern Irian Jaya where leaders of several clan groups hold customary ownership rights to the forest. YLS entered the villages' forest areas in mid-1989 and agreed to the leaders' demands for compensation in cash and in kind. But soon afterward, YLS began cutting in the village forests without paying the agreed compensation. Villagers also complained that the logging operations were damaging rattan resources and ruining hunting, an important local source of subsistence. One villager's story encapsulates the problem:

> "On the way to see Pedu, head of my clan, [a representative of the timber company] was surprised to find a very big Agathis tree. He asked me who owned the tree and

the forest. I told him it belonged to me. He asked how much was the tree and if I wanted to sell it to him. I said two million rupiah [$1000]. With a surprised look, he said that it was too expensive, that he could not afford it, but that he would cut it down in the future anyway. I told him he could not do it unless he paid the two million rupiah. He replied that he had paid five *billion* rupiah to the governor and the head of Jayapura district, so he had the right to cut the tree. I said that the governor and the district head were Sentani and Tobati people and, therefore, he could go to Sentani and Tobati and cut their trees." (Tjitradjaja, 1991)

While some timber firms negotiate informal settlements with *adat* forest landowners, many establish their claim by fiat. In Central Sulawesi, for example, a logging firm claimed local farmlands as part of their concession area, destroyed crops to plant timber species, and posted signs prohibiting tree cutting and crop cultivation and threatening violators with 10-year prison sentences or fines of up to Rp. 100 million [$50,000]. (WALHI, 1993)

In some cases, disputes between *adat* landowners and development projects have turned violent. *(See Boxes 2.1 and 2.2.)* In Pulau Panggung in the Lampung province of Sumatra, local communities were informed in early 1988 that their crops (mostly coffee) and homes were illegally sited on state forest lands slated for reforestation. They were given the choice of joining a resettlement program in another province or buying private land on their own outside of the designated Forest Area. While some residents willingly signed up for the resettlement program, various restrictions on participation and allegations of extortion by local officials soon brought the registration process to a halt. Between November 1988 and June 1989, according to investigations of the Indonesian Legal Aid Institute, local officials took matters in their own hands: over 500 homes were ransacked or burned, hundreds of coffee trees were destroyed, coffee-hulling and other machinery was demolished, and tons of dried coffee beans were confiscated or burned. The local

Box 2.1. Forest Tenure Conflict in Lampung, Sumatra

Lampung province is located on the southern tip of Sumatra, less than two hours by ferry from the western tip of Java. It owes its high rural population density of 126/km^2 (in 1986)—the highest in Indonesia outside of Java and Bali—to nine decades of heavy migration from Java, both planned and spontaneous. In the demographic shift, the native Lampung people have become a minority, outnumbered by the Javanese population.

Lampung is also one of Indonesia's most deforested provinces, with remnant forest cover of only 19 percent. Remaining forest areas are degraded and overrun—virtually no forest areas are free of settlers. Provincial forestry officials estimate that some 85,000 people live in protected forests alone.

To government, these forest settlers possess no legal right to the land they occupy and degrade. Its solution has been to resettle some 48,000 of them on non-forest lands, often through use of military force, through the "local transmigration scheme." Villages have been burned, and recalcitrant villagers imprisoned. Some resisters, however, claim that they hold valid rights to the forest lands under customary law, and observers have noted that the way these villagers use the land may be ecologically superior to planting fast-growing trees of a single species—the government approach.

In the heart of Lampung lies Gunung Balak, a roughly 20,000-hectare watershed that has been designated as Protection Forest since the colonial era and that now feeds an irrigation project. To provide extra catchment protection for a 7,000-hectare irrigation expansion downstream, the Ministry of Forestry gazetted an additional 4,500 hectares to the catchment area in 1984. The government's position has been that the settlers' land uses are degrading the watershed and hurting other conservation objectives, and that they must be removed from the land

so that it may be "regreened" as a protection forest zone. Part of this land was claimed under customary land rights by villagers in Way Abar, descendants of Javanese origin who settled the land in 1932 in accordance with valid local customary tenurial procedures.

When the provincial government instructed the people of Way Abar to move to a new area, they refused, partly because neighbors who had been relocated to the same new area had found it much less fertile than Way Abar, watched their standard of living erode, and suffered near-famine conditions. Taking their case to court, the villagers argued unsuccessfully that if they had to be moved, the government should follow the land acquisition and compensation procedures of the Basic Agrarian Law of 1960 (which applies to tenurial matters on non-forest lands), not those of the Basic Forestry Law of 1967 (under which they held no rights whatsoever.)

This socially divisive resettlement scheme can't be justified on grounds of forest or watershed protection. The catchment's average slope is less than 10 percent, so depopulating the area doesn't make sense as an erosion-control measure. Moreover, almost 70 percent of the area was green—mostly a multi-storied agroforestry system of coffee, annual crops, and as many as 63 local varieties of fruit and other trees. Villagers also seemed willing to modify their agricultural practices to better preserve the watershed. In contrast, the lands left by neighboring villagers who were resettled have been stripped of fruit trees and replanted with a monoculture of *Albizia falcataria*. Even under optimal growing conditions, these areas will need at least four to seven years to attain the same level of vegetative cover that the "encroachers" of Way Abar achieved. Given population pressures in the area, resentment of the government's policy, and the limited patrol capacity of the forestry
continued on next page

military commander temporarily put a stop to the destruction, but the attacks began again several months later. (YLBHI, 1989) The Pulau Panggung case is not representative of government policy, but it illustrates what can happen when local community rights are not recognized, legally designated forest areas aren't effectively protected, and local government cannot easily be held accountable to local communities for its actions. It may also signal conflicts to come, as pressures for both development and conservation increase.

To be fair, forestry law and policy are not the only forces undermining traditional *adat* systems of social organization and resource management. Increasing exposure to development programs, the commercial economy, the mass media, and external contacts of all types can tear communities apart.

Jurisdictional problems are also compounded by the sheer speed with which the central government has transformed the tenurial landscape over vast areas of thinly-settled and administered forest territories. While logging concessions, for example, may by law be issued only in areas classified as Production or Conversion Forest, in practice they have overlapped Protection Forest and Nature Reserve areas. (GOI, 1991) One recent study concludes that "collusive agreements between officials of the Forestry Department and concessionaires, inadequate mapping, tardy gazetting of nature reserves, and poor coordination among authorities controlling each use category resulted in the transfer of 4.55 million hectares of protection and conservation forests to HPHs by 1990." (WALHI/LBH, 1992)

Even where legal concessions do not overlap with protected forests, illegal, out-of-boundaries logging in all categories of protected forests, including National Parks, is common. (WALHI, 1993a; Callister, 1992; Dick, 1991) Small wonder: one study notes, "*...despite many violations, frequently documented in the press, no logging company has ever been prosecuted for illegal felling of trees on a reserve.*" [Emphasis in original.] (RePPProt, 1990) Lack of reliable basic data also undermines sound management. By 1984, more than 15 years after concession rights leasing began, less than one percent of all concessionaires had submitted the aerial photographs required for planning and controlling logging operations. (Gunawan, 1991)

On balance then, national forestry law and these other pressures have together turned what could have been a gradual process of *adat* adaption and cooperation with government and the private sector into a rapid slide toward open access, ecological degradation, and social conflict.

Unbalanced Rights and Responsibilities in Production Forests

Another tenurial problem in Indonesia's forests revolves around the balance of rights and correlative duties transferred to logging concession-holders. To enforce the obligations mandated by law, financial, human, and technological resources would have to increase by at least an order of magnitude. Even then, the resulting management improvements would not guarantee the forests' sustainability.

Concession-holders are legally bound to prepare and adhere to an approved management plan, mark concession boundaries, conduct a pre-harvest inventory, develop roads and other infrastructure, provide facilities for workers, follow the approved cutting system (TPTI), and take numerous other actions. But the Ministry of Forestry estimated in 1990 that only about 4 percent of

Yamdena is a small coral island of 535,000 hectares, situated in Indonesia's Tanimbar Islands in Maluku Province. So valuable are its varied moist, dry monsoon, and savanna forests, that in 1971 the government decreed the whole island a protected forest and research area, expressly prohibiting commercial forestry. But in April 1991, HPH logging rights to exploit 164,000 of Yamdena's 172,000 hectares of forest were granted to P.T. Alam Nusa Segar (ANS) by the Ministry of Forestry. Logging began in January 1992, raising a storm of protest from the island's people, who claimed that ANS had not consulted the community and that no prior notice was given that a HPH license was to be issued. Islanders brought their protests to the national Parliament in July, but logging continued.

On September 9, 1992, some 400 local islanders attacked ANS' barracks and camps, one person was killed, and several people were injured. Some 39 people were arrested, and by some accounts were beaten with rifle butts. The Bishop of Maluku Province sent strong letters of protest to the government, asserting that government troops "acted with iron hands and extra-judicially against the people they are supposed to protect."

The Ministry of Forestry now recognizes the costs of the Yamdena situation, and in late-1992 it froze all timber operations on the island for six months, pending the outcome of an environmental review. In early 1993, the new Minister reaffirmed the freeze, saying that the decision on whether logging would continue at the end of the six-month moratorium would be determined on the basis of the local communities' wishes after public consultations with them. A Commission of the Indonesian Parliament returned from a late August 1993 fact-finding trip to Yamdena to recommend that the logging freeze be lifted, as it was hurting the local economy. At the same time, representatives of a local NGO, the Tanimbar Intellectuals' Association (ICTI), continued to argue that continued logging would spell environmental disaster. The Minister nevertheless decided to lift the freeze, albeit with a likely reduction in the concession's cutting area to be announced after "further studies." In addition, state-owned corporations and cooperatives are to be phased into partial ownership of the ANS concession, a move that will make participation by local inhabitants in the company a priority, according to the Minister. ICTI remains opposed to the resumption of logging, which would probably damage the island's fragile environment and fracture its social peace.

Sources: Jakarta Post 1993c, 1993d, 1993e; B. Aji 1993.

concession-holders were fully complying with applicable regulations (Callister, 1992), though the Minister in 1993 ranked only 13 percent as "mismanaged," and estimated that some 25 percent are "well-managed." (Suharyanto, 1993) One more recent field study of five concessions in different parts of the country found evidence that in every concession, boundaries were manipulated, log production volume and production costs were falsified, undersized and riverine trees were cut, roads were poorly built, ebony was illegally exported, Protection Forest and other areas outside authorized cutting blocks were logged, and excessive damage was done to residual stands during harvesting. (WALHI 1993a) A 1992 Asian Development Bank team appraising a proposed biodiversity-conservation project observed that on the Sumatran island of Siberut:

Commercial logging concessions cover most of the island and timber cutting has transgressed protected area boundaries in several locations. Logging near rivers, watercourses and steep slopes is common and no refor- estation programs on logged-over forest areas have been initiated. The soils…are un- suitable for commercial logging and prone to severe erosion. (ADB 1992)

In Siberut, the national government is phasing out all logging activities by 1994. But a total ban is obviously not viable for the whole of Indone- sia's forests.

Beginning around 1989, the Ministry of Fores- try began to crack down on violators, and as of 1991 it had revoked about 42 HPH contracts, and suspended 53. Some 380 fines totalling more than $20 million were imposed on roughly 270 conces- sion-holders. As of March 1993, the Ministry had collected some $12.8 million, and was still wait- ing for the remaining $10.6 million. (Suharyanto, 1993) Few outside government know, though, which concessions were fined for what violations, and which ones have paid. One of the largest fines, which was widely publicized—$5.6 million levied against P.T. Barito Pacific for illegal log- ging in a Kalimantan protected area and on an adjoining concession between 1985 and 1988— was subsequently reduced to $4.2 million, and as of late 1991 the firm was still disputing the allega- tions and withholding payment. (Callister, 1992) The one concession-holder who appealed revoca- tion of his license in Administrative Court won the case, because the Ministry did not have ade- quate data to prove the violations. (WALHI, 1993a)

Given the large profits that concession-holders can expect, they may view the current level of fines and compliance with stepped-up enforce- ment as merely another cost of doing business rather than as a strong deterrent. In any case, the current grab-bag of responses to the problem—a wide range of technical and bureaucratic require- ments that are difficult for the government to monitor—isn't enough. Current concession regu- lations aren't oriented toward monitoring and maintaining the forest's ecological functions and biological diversity or toward improving the so- cial and economic welfare of forest communities.

Directions and Strategies for Change

Four changes are needed in Indonesia's tenur- ial system to support a more sustainable and equitable future for the nation's forests:

1. The enforcement of concession-holders' re- sponsibilities under their contracts through intensified monitoring, higher fines, and broader sanctions, perhaps coupled with the requirement that concession-holders post and keep replenished a stiff performance bond that the government could draw on when the evaluations of an independent and credible monitoring entity reveal violations;

2. The cancellation or phase-out of concessions that conflict with or threaten designated protected areas, areas ecologically unsuited to logging, and forests that established local communities depend upon for a significant share of their livelihoods;

3. The demarcation and legal recognition of customary *adat* land and resource rights in areas where communities are willing to work with government and others to man- age forest resources sustainably; and

4. The reconfiguration of production forest areas into permanent production units with boundaries supported by all local land- users and some form of profit-sharing with local communities who lose access to re- sources in concession areas.

Some government policy-makers have become more receptive to these proposals in the past few years, and some innovative preliminary actions have been taken. Besides the recent step-up in en- forcement noted above, the government is also beginning to correct the often vague and inaccu- rate results of the province-by-province Consen- sus Forest Land Use Planning (TGHK) process carried out in the early 1980s.

One promising initiative, known as the KPHP system, is being tested by the Ministry of Forestry in the provinces of Central Kalimantan and Jambi (Sumatra), with support from the British Overseas Development Administration. Under a 1991 Ministerial Decree,[11] the KPHP (Production Forest Utilization Units) are established as the smallest units of forest that can be managed on sustainable principles. The hope is that KPHPs will be an ecologically and economically rational unit of permanent production forest, bounded by natural features and roads whenever possible and recognized by all land-users in the vicinity. From a tenurial standpoint, the key features are that boundaries "must be subject to a negotiation with local communities" and that "boundary changes will be inevitable." (ODA 1993) The Ministry might even channel some percentage of revenues derived from logging activities directly to communities who lose access to forest lands in the KPHP.

Other developments should help clarify tenurial status too. In the Production Forests, the Association of Indonesian Forest Industries (APHI) is conducting a 5-year aerial mapping at 1:20,000 for all forest concessions and, as of mid-1993, some 62 million hectares had been covered by remote sensing, and 35 million hectares of that area had been interpreted, at a cost of $100 million. Meanwhile, in a pilot effort, the Forestry Ministry has contracted two private firms to design a new concession-monitoring system and to establish a new entity to audit and inspect concession operations. (WALHI, 1993a)

Government policy on the rights of traditional *adat* communities in the forest may be on the verge of changing as well. The 1992 Law on Population Development and Family Welfare recognizes the right of "vulnerable peoples" to "utilize a customary territorial heritage, as well as the right to preserve or develop the behavior of cultural life."[12] The official Elucidation of this Law leaves little doubt that a dramatic departure from the Basic Forestry Law and other past policies toward traditional forest communities' land rights is now at least possible:

The rights to utilize local customary territorial heritage provide a guarantee that groups of people who have traditionally developed

an area for generations will not be overwhelmed by newcomers. If such a local customary territorial heritage is developed for development activities, the original inhabitants shall be given a priority to enjoy the enhanced value of their territory, for example through new job opportunities and so forth…

The rights to preserve and develop the behavior of cultural life covers physical aspects (relating to land) and non-physical aspects…tribes or groups which have special ways of behavior cannot be forced to change their ways of life to conform with others. Such changes must be in accordance with the development which they themselves have chosen.

How conflicts are to be resolved is not specified. Still, even if read only as a statement of policy-makers' changing perceptions, it paves the way for recognizing local rights in forest lands and resources and for constructing durable forest-management partnerships between the state and the community. Indeed, in April 1993, the newly installed Minister of Forestry said that "*adat* rights should be utilized to support national development in the forestry sector to the maximum extent possible." (Neraca, 1993)

Building on these nascent shifts in policy and legal foundations, positive examples and pilot projects are needed to illustrate concretely how recognizing local forest land and resource rights can benefit not only the community, but also the state and the private sector. Recent research in Kalimantan involving cooperation between the Ministry of Forestry and Indonesian and U.S. university researchers provides evidence that partnerships between government and local communities may be the key to regenerating disturbed rainforest. (Abdoellah et al. 1993) In the areas studied, villagers have been unable to control access to or protect their forest and land resources amid well-financed government development programs and commercial operations. Still, the active involvement and support of officials from the Ministry in this effort is a hopeful sign.

Another small-scale but potentially important initiative is taking place in the Sanggau region of West Kalimantan, where a Ministry of Forestry project combines agroforestry development with a new pilot "community forest concession." Supported by a grant from the German government, the project combines fieldwork with the creation of a policy group, the "Commission for Development of Community Forests," in the Ministry. The project will run at least eight to ten years—enough time for strong local, provincial, and national institutions to develop. (Departamen Kehutanan 1991) What sets this project apart from others of its kind is the Ministry of Forestry's willingness to at least look at different tenurial systems in forests.

These and similar initiatives are signs that policy-makers in Indonesia are taking a cautious second look at the forest tenurial regime that has prevailed for the past several decades, with an eye to revising the concession system and at least partially recognizing traditional rights and management systems. Getting beyond pilot projects and well-intended policy statements, however, means making changes in the larger political economy and policy-making apparatus that has shaped the forestry sector and constrained change. *(See Chapters III and IV.)*

Forest Tenure in the United States

In June 1992, NASA's Goddard Space Flight Center released satellite images comparing forests in the state of Amazonas in Brazil to forests in Mt. Hood National Forest in Oregon. (Eagan, 1992) While the Amazonas forest was largely undisturbed, except where the forest edges had been rolled back by logging and agriculture along roads, the Oregon image showed a forest fragmented by hundreds of clearcuts. Mature forest was confined almost entirely to small blocks scattered across the landscape and to narrow strips along highways (Potemkin forests that create the illusion that motorists are driving through large expanses of mature forest).

To the northwest, across the Columbia River, the forests of southwestern Washington are almost entirely in forest-industry hands. The landscape there takes on a more uniform appearance—a green carpet of young Douglas firs—since there is no old-growth forest and little forest older than 30 to 40 years left to fragment. The forest still produces timber and a shrinking number of jobs, but it no longer sustains the prodigious runs of salmon, steelhead, and sturgeon that once spawned in its streams. By the same token, many other species once found in abundance in the rich coastal forests are now rare or gone. (Norse, 1990)

In the Pacific Northwest, "sustainable" forest management is in trouble on federal, state, corporate, and individually owned lands. In many ways, these troubles stem from economic and political factors. *(See Chapters III and IV.)* But tenurial factors doubtless complicate the transition to more ecologically sound forest management.

On the one hand, the rights and responsibilities of forest owners in the Northwest are defined in ways that protect forest resources much better than less explicit tenurial systems can. For instance, U.S. laws guaranteeing private property owners the continued use of their lands into the indefinite future is one key to sustainable management, and the laws establishing national parks and wilderness areas on federal lands protect natural forest ecosystems that might otherwise be destroyed. On the other hand, the laws governing tenurial relationships, often based on traditional approaches to forestry, have undercut forest values and functions across the Pacific Northwest. On both public and private lands, timber-dominated forest management reduces the average age of forests, makes them less diverse, and takes a toll on fisheries, endangered species, water quality, and recreation.

Recognizing these problems, forestry researchers and a small but growing band of professional foresters are seeking to develop new approaches[13] to forest management. *(See Box 2.3.)* Variously referred to as forest ecosystem management and "new forestry," these approaches seek to maintain the forest's ecological and economic diversity by changing silvicultural practices and maintaining late successional forests. The strong

Box 2.3. New Forestry

As chief forest ecologist for the U.S. Forest Service in the Pacific Northwest, Jerry Franklin spent over 25 years pushing the frontiers of ecological knowledge. During the 1970s and early 1980s, Franklin and a group of his colleagues at the agency's research station in Corvallis, Oregon, characterized forest ecosystems in the Northwest and studied their composition, structure, and functions to learn how they regenerated and renewed themselves, especially in response to fire and other severe natural disturbances. (e.g., Franklin et al., 1981) What the team discovered about old-growth forest ecosystems upset much of the conventional wisdom about their value. They are highly variable and biologically diverse, and they leave a legacy of structural diversity and organic productivity in younger forests for decades after most of the old trees succumb to windstorms, fires, insects, or disease.

In the early 1980s, Franklin and his colleagues began to turn their attention to forest management. A few years later, backed by research at the H.J. Andrews Experimental Forest in Oregon, they started to urge foresters and all other takers to re-examine conventional silvicultural wisdom in the Northwest. For decades, convention has dictated that clearcuts, intensive burning of post-harvest woody debris ("slash"), and soil scarification (exposure) were the best techniques for regenerating Douglas fir in the Pacific Northwest. Franklin's group, however, argued that forest managers must learn to better mimic the complexity of natural forest stands for the sake of biodiversity, fisheries habitats, and, ultimately, the health of the forest. (e.g., Franklin and Forman, 1987) This approach to forest management eventually came to be known as New Forestry.

How New Forestry differs from conventional forest management in the Northwest depends on who you ask. Three general principles are agreed upon, however. First, New Forestry means leaving clusters of large green trees in harvest areas that will slowly age with the younger stand around it to provide the dead snags and rotting logs needed to conserve biodiversity. (How many and where provide much of the grist for debates over New Forestry.) It also means leaving downed logs in harvested areas, since the rotting wood serves as nurseries for many tree seedlings that cannot compete with herbaceous plants on the forest floor, and allowing substantial amounts of wood to collect in streams to provide habitats for riparian organisms. Second, reversing the current trend, New Forestry seeks to extend rotation lengths to between 80 and 120 years, and perhaps more. Third, harvest patterns are planned on a landscape scale to preserve connections between forest stands of various ages and to maximize the contiguous area of older stands.

New Forestry has critics on both sides of the forestry reform debate. (Gregg, 1991) Those who believe that forestry works well as currently practiced see little "new" in New Forestry and claim that many of its techniques have been used in the past and found to be less effective than clearcutting and intensive soil preparation. (e.g., Atkinson, 1990) At the other extreme, some critics don't think New Forestry goes far enough. They believe its loose definition allows foresters to leave a few standing trees and a snag or two in the middle of a large clearcut and call it New Forestry. And if rotation lengths aren't extended to between 200 and 400 years, some suspect that New Forestry will simply create slightly cluttered, older tree plantations. Many critics also fear that New Forestry will be invoked to justify logging in unprotected old-growth forests.

Whatever the fate of New Forestry, it has drawn the spotlight to the importance of grounding forest management in ecological
(continued on next page)

understanding. Along with other approaches to forest ecosystem management, it has received attention from the Forest Service's controversial New Perspectives Program, established in the late 1980s to promote experimentation and the integration of non-timber values in forest management.[1]

In June 1992, the Forest Service announced that it will practice forest ecosystem management on most of its timberlands and will sharply reduce clearcutting. Exactly how the ecosystem management policy will be implemented remains to be seen, but the emergence of New Forestry (and other similar approaches) and ecosystem management policies adopted by federal and state agencies indicate the increasing role that ecology, public participation, and true long-term planning will play in American forest management.

---

1. Critics of New Perspectives (and the new U.S. Forest Service forest ecosystem management policy) assert it is being used as an excuse to log the largest remaining unprotected roadless primary forests in the biologically diverse Siskiyou Mountains in Southwest Oregon. (e.g., Kerr, 1990)

---

assertion of private property rights, however, makes restructuring and coordinating forest rights and responsibilities at an ecologically significant scale complicated. The historical evolution of public land ownership under various legal definitions of private access and public administrative control has also been an obstacle. So far, the way forest resources are legally defined, used, and maintained has been out of sync with rapidly changing scientific and social views of forest values.

Forest Ownership, Rights and Responsibilities in the Pacific Northwest

In the United States, authority and responsibility over forest resources is relatively decentralized. Federal, state, and local governments and private forest owners all have well recognized and clearly defined authority over the use of forest lands. The U.S. Constitution's Fifth and Fourteenth Amendments[14] protect private property owners from government usurpation[15] or competing private claims, while governmental regulatory authority over private lands derives from common law and legal doctrines that have established that private property owners cannot use their property in a way that will harm the property of others.[16] Public forest lands are governed by various legislative acts.

The most important determinant of tenurial rights and responsibilities over forest lands is ownership. Nationwide, nearly two-thirds (64 percent) of forest lands are privately owned while the remainder (36 percent) is controlled by public agencies. (USDA, 1989) The federal government, the largest single owner of forest lands, administers nearly 101 million hectares, or approximately 35 percent of all U.S. forests, most of it located in the Rocky Mountain and Pacific Coast states and Alaska.[17] *(See Figure 2.1.)*

Oregon and Washington together have approximately 19.9 million hectares of forest lands. (Waddell, et al., 1989) Ownership patterns on these lands were largely determined in the late nineteenth and early twentieth centuries. *(See Box 2.4 and Figure 2.2.)* Today, some 57 percent of all forests are on federal lands, and 7 percent are on state and local government lands. Privately held forests account for 36 percent of the total forested area; of this, 62 percent belongs to the forest industry and 38 percent to small private, non-industrial owners. (MacLean et al. 1992; Bassett and Oswald 1983; Gedney et al. 1989; 1987; 1986a; 1986b) *(See Figure 2.3.)*

Private Forest Lands

Private forest lands in the Pacific Northwest—most of them west of the Cascades—total 6.9 million hectares. Roughly 4.3 million hectares are owned by the forest industry while the remainder is controlled by non-industrial or small private

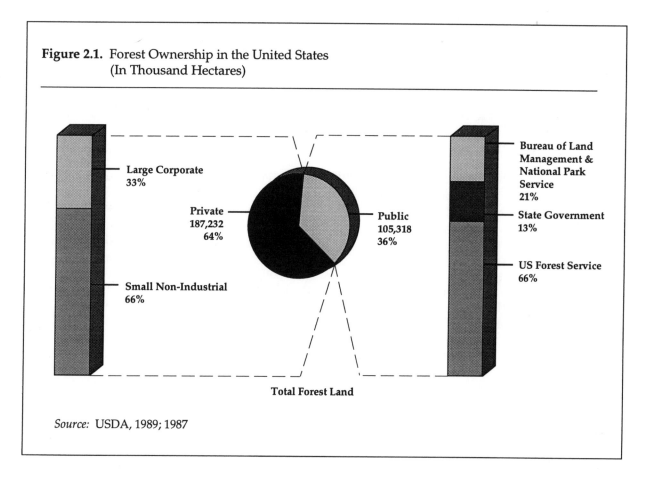

Figure 2.1. Forest Ownership in the United States
(In Thousand Hectares)

Large Corporate
33%

Private
187,232
64%

Small Non-Industrial
66%

Public
105,318
36%

Bureau of Land
Management &
National Park
Service
21%

State Government
13%

US Forest Service
66%

Total Forest Land

Source: USDA, 1989; 1987

landowners.[18] (MacLean et al. 1992; Gedney et al. 1989, 1987, 1986a, 1986b; Bassett and Oswald, 1983) Forest-industry timberlands in the Northwest are concentrated in the Olympic Peninsula, southwestern Washington, the Oregon Coast Range, and in the western foothills of the Cascades.

Except in extremely limited circumstances,[19] the constitutional basis for private property rights in the United States—in force for over 200 years and unlikely to change any time soon—allows private forest owners to reserve exclusive (though not necessarily absolute) rights to forest resources on their lands.[20] Rather than narrowing private property rights to protect forest resources on private lands, private forest owners' correlative duties or responsibilities have been stressed. These efforts are based on the longstanding doctrine of waste and the common law of private

nuisance. The first implies that owners may use their land in any way they please as long as they do not damage or destroy it—generally interpreted in the United States to mean that owners should do nothing to reduce property values significantly.[21] (Cubbage and Siegal, 1985) The second establishes that individuals cannot use their property in a way that will injure the property rights of others or endanger the public's health, safety, morals, and general welfare. (Roberts, 1974)

No attempt was made to regulate private forestry until the early 1900s. Most early efforts failed, and attempts led by Gifford Pinchot in the 1920s and 1930s to bring forest management practices on private forest lands under federal regulation faltered, as did several efforts in the 1940s and 1950s. (Clary, 1986) But state governments did begin to pass laws regulating forest practices

Box 2.4. The Evolution of Forest Ownership in the United States Pacific Northwest

In 1846, the United States and Great Britain settled a half-century territorial dispute over lands west of the Rockies and north of California. Under the Oregon Compromise, the federal domain of the United States expanded by 722,600 km^2 to encompass territory that would eventually become Washington, Oregon, Idaho, and parts of Montana and Wyoming. (Wyant, 1982) Of the 406,737 km^2 that eventually became Oregon and Washington, at least 40 percent was forested. Most of this forest land was found between the crest of the Cascade Range and the Pacific Ocean in a 140,000 km^2 swath extending from the California border to the Canadian frontier. These lands contained the most productive, diverse, and imposing coniferous forests in the world.

Over the next 50 years, large and small parcels of forest lands in the Pacific Northwest were transferred from the federal domain to state and private ownership. Most of it was transferred through direct sales to individuals and corporations—for many years, the going price was $2.50 an acre—or in the form of land grants to the states. Lesser amounts were transferred to individuals through the Homestead Act of 1862 and the Mining Act of 1872. The transfer of these lands conveyed absolute rights to their surface resources, including timber, and few if any land-use obligations were attached to the rights.

The largest transfers took place under legislation enacted in 1864 to provide incentives for the Northern Pacific Railroad Company to build a railroad from Duluth, Minnesota to Tacoma, Washington and Portland, Oregon. For every mile of line built in a state, the railroad received 20 square miles (5,120 hectares) of land—and 40 square miles in U.S. territories (which Washington was until 1889). Northern Pacific was also allowed to select its lands from a strip that averaged a hundred miles wide. (Wyant, 1982) Of the roughly 2.5 million hectares of forest lands in western Washington and Oregon that were transferred to the railroad in this way, many were later sold off by the railroad to timber companies. For example, in 1900 Northern Pacific sold 360,000 hectares at $15/hectare to Frederick Weyerhauser, a German immigrant who had made his fortunes in the white-pine forests of Minnesota and Wisconsin. (Wyant, 1982)

Today, at least a dozen forest-products companies in the region have major land holdings that were first owned by Northern Pacific. But in the 1870s and 1880s, as the timber industry first developed in the Pacific Northwest, there was little incentive to own private forest lands since the use of public forest lands was virtually unregulated. The devastating results of such open access in the Northwest and in other parts of the country soon spawned a debate over the disposal of federal lands. A movement began to set aside some public lands for future timber reserves and conservation. Eventually, 8.3 million hectares of public forest lands in Washington and Oregon were incorporated into the National Forest system administered by the U.S. Forest Service. Most of the remaining federal forest lands in the Northwest were eventually placed under the management of the Bureau of Land Management (1 million hectares) and the National Park Service (850,000 hectares).

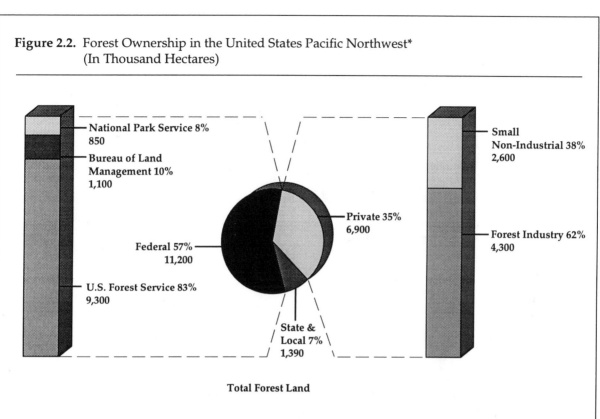

Figure 2.2. Forest Ownership in the United States Pacific Northwest*
(In Thousand Hectares)

National Park Service 8%
850

Bureau of Land
Management 10%
1,100

Federal 57%
11,200

U.S. Forest Service 83%
9,300

Private 35%
6,900

State &
Local 7%
1,390

Small
Non-Industrial 38%
2,600

Forest Industry 62%
4,300

Total Forest Land

Source: MacLean, et al, 1992; Waddell, et al, 1989; Gedney, et al, 1986a, 1989; Basset & Oswald, 1983
* States of Oregon and Washington

on private and on state and local government-owned forest lands. Between 1937 and 1955, fifteen states passed forest practices acts with limited provisions, including Oregon in 1941 and Washington in 1945. (Cubbage and Siegel, 1985) These early laws were limited in scope (usually requiring steps to reduce fire hazard or to replant), poorly enforced, and in some cases compliance was voluntary. But in the early 1970s, Oregon and Washington revised their forest laws to address a wider scope of issues with more stringent provisions. Supported by most forest land-owners concerned about overlapping and conflicting regulation by numerous state and local agencies (Salazar and Cubbage, 1990), these laws (along with California's) are now considered the country's most comprehensive. Even so, they are primarily intended to maximize timber

production while secondarily protecting water resources and endangered species.

Oregon's forest-practices legislation typifies private forest-land regulation in both states. The Oregon State Forest Practices Act[22] regulates forest operations on private and state forest lands through the implementation of administrative rules developed by the State Forestry Board. Administered by the State Forester and the Oregon Department of Forestry, these rules are intended to promote reforestation, protect water quality in streams and wetlands, and conserve sensitive habitats for endangered species. *(See Box 2.5.)* Harvest rates or volumes are not regulated, and the regulations do not cover the location of clearcuts, except in riparian and wetland areas or "special resource" sites.[23]

Figure 2.3. Forest Cover and Federal Lands in the Pacific Northwest

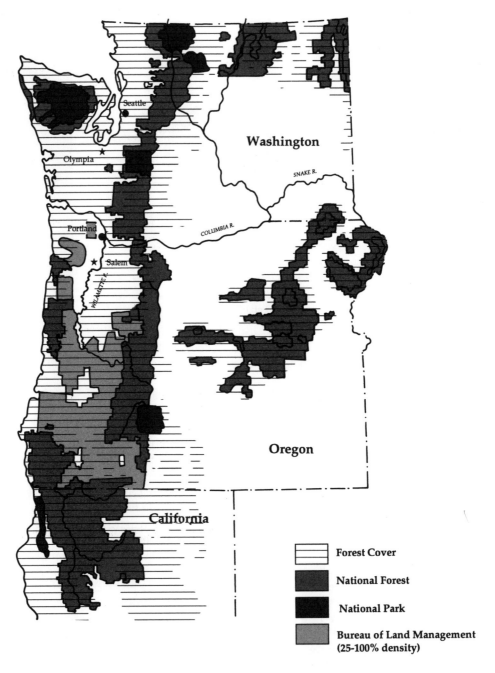

Forest Cover

National Forest

National Park

Bureau of Land Management
(25-100% density)

Source: U.S. Department of Agriculture, Forest Service – 1989; 1983 and Wilderness Society, 1991

Box 2.5. The Oregon State Forest Practices Act

The Oregon State Forest Practices Act applies to all private forest lands in the state that are used for "production forestry."[1] The regulations are formulated for each of the forestry department's four administrative regions to account for ecological differences between regions. But all four sets of regulations require forest owners (or operators on private forest lands) to notify the State Forester before operations begin and prohibit clearcuts larger than 240 contiguous acres (96 hectares).[2] The state forest practice rules also require a minimal level of replanting on clearcut lands within two years, and include general regulations on the use of chemicals and the placement and construction of roads. (Cubbage, et al., 1993) In 1991, based on the emerging principles of "New Forestry" *(see Box 2.3),* a provision in force until 1995 was passed requiring owners to leave an average of five live trees or snags and five downed logs or trees per hectare on any clearcut larger than four hectares.

More specific provisions of the Oregon State Forest Practices Act regulate forest practices in river and stream areas, near wetlands, and near resource sites specified by other laws or the state forester, such as habitats for endangered species. (Oregon Department of Forestry, 1991) Within a narrow strip along wetlands (100 meters), and streams, rivers, and lakes (30 meters), forest owners must take specific steps to protect shade cover and fish and wildlife habitat. The use of herbicides and pesticides on these strips is also regulated, though not necessarily prohibited. Before logging in such areas, the owner must provide the state forester with a management plan specifying how the rules will be implemented. Although these are routinely approved, the state forester may reject plans for logging in some cases. Provisions applying to specified resource sites (among them, nesting or roosting sites for sensitive birds, sensitive habitats for threatened and endangered wildlife, and wetlands larger than 3.2 hectares) vary with the site, but in general, they impose seasonal restrictions on forest operations or require landowners to create small buffer zones. In addition, forest owners must file a management plan for operations within 100 meters of such areas for approval by the state forester.

----

1. Forest lands that are being converted to non-forest uses are exempt from the Oregon State Forest Practices Act.

2. If a clearcut is larger than 120 acres (48 hectares), it must be more than 300 feet (90 meters) from a previous clearcut, unless the previous clearcut has been reforested according to standards established by the state board of forestry.

¶ #1 esp.

The penalties for violating the Oregon State Forest Practices Act are minor. Criminal penalties are misdemeanors punishable by a maximum $1,000 fine and/or 1 year jail term, and civil penalties are limited to no more than $5,000. Although Oregon has 26 field offices and a relatively large forest-practices section in the Oregon Department of Forestry, monitoring and enforcement are limited. Compliance with the forest practices rules is basically voluntary for most forest owners, and the Oregon Department of Forestry spends most of its funds for implementing the act on education and extension to promote compliance.

Numerous federal laws may impose limited responsibilities on private forest owners. The Clean Water Act, for instance, prohibits individuals and corporations, including forest land owners, from dumping certain pollutants in rivers, lakes and wetlands, and regulates the modification or conversion of wetlands. But such laws have limited effects on most forest-management operations.

Under the Endangered Species Act, only the federal government and the state cooperate on species recovery plans. Private land owners may, however, be required to help government agencies with species recovery under Section 9 of the Act.[24] How recovery plans for several endangered species (e.g., the northern spotted owl, the grizzly bear, the marbled murrelet, and several salmon subspecies) will affect private forest owners is not yet clear. To minimize conflicts with private forest owners over such plans, the federal government has emphasized habitat protection on public lands and voluntary cooperative efforts on private lands.

Among the few incentives or obligations that private land owners have to manage forest ecosystems are those to replant logged areas and to provide limited protection for water resources and endangered species. In this sense, state forest practices legislation has worked reasonably well. Reforestation is now more successful on private lands[25] than it is on many public lands (Olson, 1988; Yoho, 1985), and water quality and critical habitats are undoubtedly better protected than they were 25 years ago. But private responsibilities are defined mainly to protect timber, and many incentives for maintaining other forest uses

and resources have yet to be defined. As a result, private forest owners have converted most of their forests to young even-aged stands, often composed of only one or two tree species. More than 70 percent of the forest-industry lands in western Washington are in even-aged stands less than 70 years old, while mixed-aged stands cover only 5 percent of the area. (MacLean, et. al, 1992) As natural forests give way to tree farms, species that flourish only in late successional forests grow rare or die out.

According to recent research (Hansen et al., 1991), even-aged forest stands—even those more than a century old—have fewer species and less abundant wildlife populations than uneven-aged natural forest ecosystems. Other research indicates that even-aged, monocultural forest stands have higher insect pest populations and fewer insect-eating predators than uneven-aged forest areas. (Showalter and Means, 1988) *(See Table 2.2.)* Researchers are also finding evidence that fires can wreak more damage in young plantations than in mature natural forests. (Perry, 1988; Agee and Huff, 1987)

With the private responsibilities of forest ownership confined largely to timber-production concerns, the entire burden of preserving biodiversity, recreational opportunities, salmon fisheries and the like has increasingly fallen on public lands. In many areas, however, salmon fisheries,

Table 2.2. Arthropod Biomass and Species Diversity in Douglas Fir Canopies of Old-growth Forests (400 years old) and Regenerating Monocultures (10 years old) in Western Oregon.

Feeding Groups	Old-growth Forest Biomass (gr/ha)	Old-growth Forest # of species	Regenerating Monoculture Biomass (gr/ha)	Regenerating Monoculture # of species
Herbivores	190	8	370	3
Predators	160	40	50	10
Others	30	18	0	2
Total	380	66	420	15

Source: Adapted from Norse (1990)

water quality, and the fate of some species will depend on how private forest lands are managed. Unless the public is willing to purchase various forest ecosystem goods and services from private forest owners just as they purchase wood products today, new regulations and, more importantly, incentives to broaden private landowner responsibilities will have to be devised to sustain many forest values across the region. Meanwhile, the transformation of natural forest ecosystems to intensively managed tree farms is likely to continue on the most productive private lands, while others are managed minimally or converted to non-forest uses.[26]

Public Forest Lands

In Oregon and Washington as in most western states, governments, (especially the federal government) are the largest owners of forest lands. Of the roughly 13 million hectares of public forests in these two states, 11.8 million hectares are owned by the federal government, and the remaining 1.2 million hectares by state and local governments.[27] In the western portion of the two states, federal ownership is concentrated in an unbroken network of National Forests in the Cascade mountains, the Olympic mountains, scattered portions of the Oregon Coast Range, and the Siskiyou mountains of southwestern Oregon. East of the Cascades, most federal forest lands are in National Forests stretching across northern Washington and parts of central and northeast Oregon. State forest lands are scattered in both states, mostly west of the Cascades.[28]

The present network of federal forest lands is rooted in the Forest Reserve Act (1891), which allowed the President to set aside public lands in forest reserves, and the Organic Act (1897), which set broad directions for their management. The Transfer Act (1905) created the U.S. Forest Service to manage most federal forest lands in the United States, including the Pacific Northwest. Most of the remaining federal forest lands in the Northwest were eventually placed under the management of the Bureau of Land Management (1 million hectares[29]) and the National Park Service (850,000 hectares[30]).

State agencies control approximately 1.1 million hectares of timberland in state forests or multiple-use areas. Most state forest land was either purchased or taken in lieu of taxes from private owners after it had been severely degraded, abandoned, or burned. (Perry and Perry, 1983) State forest lands, legislatively mandated to produce maximum revenue to support roads and schools, have been intensively managed for timber, especially in Washington.

On public lands, the rights to use forest resources and the responsibilities for maintaining them are more precisely defined, and more complicated, than they are on private lands. The federal government allocates differential use rights to the general public and to private interests in accordance with federal legislation and administrative regulations. Responsibilities and rights are construed and allocated by different government agencies in different ways. In general, the long-term sustainability of forest resources is not threatened on public forest lands where consumptive rights to forest resources are restricted. In the Northwest, these lands include designated wilderness areas (1.65 million hectares) and Research Natural Areas (less than 10,000 hectares) in National Forests, as well as National Parks (850,000 hectares), and National Wildlife Refuges (less than 5,000 hectares). These mostly high-elevation and low-yielding forests are available for a variable range of non-consumptive and limited consumptive public uses (such as hunting or fishing), but they cannot be logged. Responsibility for maintaining these areas as natural ecosystems with minimal human impact is specified in such legislation as the National Park Service Organic Act (1916), the Wilderness Act (1964), and other laws and administrative orders. With use so limited and strong laws in place, government has in general made good on its obligation to protect these forest lands.

On "multiple-use" federal forest lands, which comprise roughly 9 million hectares of federal forest lands in Oregon and Washington, balancing rights to exploit timber with legal responsibilities to protect the environment has been more difficult. (See Box 2.6.) The U.S. Forest Service and

33

Box 2.6. Federal Timber Sales

Each year, the federal government determines which forest areas are to be offered in timber sales through a complex planning process. *(See Chapter IV.)* Most such sales are of mature timber stands that are no longer growing rapidly. The amount and quality of timber in the sale area is estimated by the U.S. Forest Service or Bureau of Land Management before the timber sale. Timber sales vary in size and volume, though the size of individual clearcuts within a sale area is usually limited to 16 hectares.

Sales are conducted through sealed bids, and the rights to harvest the timber are sold to the highest bidder. Before the bidding takes place, prospective bidders will examine inventory data and then accompany government timber sale staff to the sale location where the terms and conditions of the sale are explained, after which interested parties submit bids. The timber sale contract spells out the purchaser's operational responsibilities. Typically, these responsibilities specify the boundaries of the sale area, the location of roads, the skid trail layout, the harvesting systems to be used, and post-

harvest measures to prevent erosion. Compliance with timber sale contracts is monitored by the timber sales staff of the ranger district in which the sale occurred, although the Forest Service admits that many sales are never inspected carefully enough to detect fraud or theft. (Long, 1991) Investigators from the House Appropriations Committee charge the Forest Service has not adequately monitored contract compliance which has resulted in the public losing millions in timber thefts, due in part to investigations hampered by the industry's "undue political influence" and interference from the agency's own managers. (Sonner, 1993) Still, government shoulders many of the responsibilities directly or indirectly related to timber management on federal lands. For example, road construction, maintenance, road removal after harvest and replanting and reforestation are usually paid for or carried out by the U.S. Forest Service.[1]

—————

1. If a timber sale contract specifies that the purchaser must build needed roads or reforest after harvesting, those costs are credited against the sale price.

---

the Bureau of Land Management have legal responsibilities to ensure that all forest resources— not just timber, but also wildlife, watersheds, recreation, etc.—are sustained on these federal lands. The Multiple-Use Sustained Yield Act (1960), the Endangered Species Act (1972), the Forest and Rangelands Resource Planning Act (1974), and the National Forest Management Act (1976) all specify management goals, planning procedures, and decision-making processes to ensure that multiple-use areas are managed for a wide variety of forest resources. *(See Chapter IV.)* But "multiple-use" federal forest lands have not been managed sustainably. If the ratio of timber harvests to net forest growth is any measure, the

U.S. Forest Service has failed to meet its traditional responsibility to manage forests for sustained timber yield.[31] In fact, harvest levels on the National Forests in western Oregon and Washington have been larger in relation to net timber growth than they have been on private lands: 1986 harvest levels (15.3 million m^3) on the National Forests in the region exceeded the net annual growth levels (9 million m^3) by 70 percent, while harvests on private lands exceeded net growth by 34 percent. (Waddell et al., 1989) Moreover, according to the U.S. Fish and Wildlife Service (USFWS 1990; USFWS, 1992), an estimated 3.4 million acres, or 57 percent, of the native old-growth forests on Forest Service lands in Oregon and Washington were clearcut between 1955 and 1990.

Federal forest-management failures have also put species at risk. Although the northern spotted owl and marbled murrelet symbolize the clash over federal forest management, many other species have also borne the cumulative brunt of inappropriate forest practices during the past several decades. For example, a scientific panel composed of U.S.F.S. and B.L.M. biologists convened to consider management options for old-growth forests found that 48 species closely associated with old-growth forests are now at moderate or high risk of extinction or extirpation during the next 100 years. (Thomas et al., 1993) If logging proceeds as outlined in current National Forest Management Plans, the so-called Thomas report claims 294 species will be in this category.

Even the most prominent symbol of the Pacific Northwest—the salmon—has had its spawning and nursery habitats in rivers and streams in National Forests throughout the region severely damaged or destroyed, principally by logging and related road construction.[32] Between 1935 and 1992, the number of large, deep pools (critical habitat for salmonid species) on 412 miles of monitored streams in Washington and Oregon's National Forests declined by 60 percent. (Thomas, et al., 1993) The Thomas report describes the condition of stream habitats and aquatic ecosystems in general as poor on National Forests in western Oregon and Washington, and panel members consider extensive restoration efforts necessary to maintain the viability of 112 major fish stocks —some of them potentially eligible for protection under the Endangered Species Act—that depend on drainages on federal forest lands.

While most of the failure to meet legal responsibilities to manage public forest resources sustainably can be linked to economic pressures and to the policy-making process itself, weaknesses in tenurial relationships on public lands are also important. Well-intentioned provisions in various tenure-related laws have led to extremely damaging forest-management practices. For example,

after extensive clearcuts in the Bitterroots and elsewhere during the late 1960s and early 1970s, the National Forest Management Act was passed to require clearcuts to be dispersed. But even this strategy's proponents now realize that is a recipe for fragmentation and diminished biodiversity. (Sample, 1993)

dealing w/ that we don't understand

The federal government's lack of foresight may be an even more important reason behind the mis-management of public forests. As Congress piled more and more responsibility over a period of decades on the Forest Service, it failed to recognize that at some point, the nature and size of access rights to timber harvests would have to be reconciled with the growing need to maintain other resources. By not limiting rights to harvest timber on federal lands, both Congress and the Executive branch have allowed the degradation of many forest resources they have a legal obligation to protect. *(See Chapter IV.)* Unless users' rights are balanced with users' responsibilities, the list of threatened forest resources can only grow. Then, warns Secretary of Interior Bruce Babbitt, the political "train wreck" created by listing the northern spotted owl will be repeated and leave fewer forest-management options in the future. (Cohn and Williams, 1993) As more species end up on the endangered species list, habitat conservation plans will restrict forest management activities on larger parts of the public, and eventually the private, forest landscape.

Balancing Rights and Responsibilities

Ecological approaches to forest management in the Pacific Northwest can't be implemented until sound management is redefined to include practices aimed at sustaining a broad array of forest resources—not simply timber. The process is beginning, in some cases with industry support.[33] Washington state recently revised its forest practices Act to more strictly control the watershed effects of logging,[34] while the Forest Service's recent pledges to pursue forest ecosystem management, as well as the follow-up to the White House-sponsored "forest summit" held in April 1993, indicate a growing recognition that forests provide far more than trees.

Perhaps more important, efforts to create economic and policy incentives to manage all forest resources responsibly are beginning to receive attention. *(See Chapter III.)* For example, a number of West Coast organizations have developed criteria for assessing the relative sustainability of forest management. Using these criteria, they seek to "certify" sustainably produced forest products—for which they expect consumers to pay a premium. (Johnson and Cabarle, 1993)

Of course, the definition of sustainable forest management will not evolve painlessly. Individuals and institutions will try to maximize their rights and minimize their responsibilities—witness the recent surge in legal actions by private interests claiming that land-use restrictions on private lands, and limitations on private access to public resources, violate "established and inalienable rights."[35] (Gottlieb, 1989) The "Wise Use" movement seeks not only to preserve and expand private rights to natural resources but also to diminish private (and public) responsibilities to maintain them. *(See Box 2.7.)* Such conflicts won't be resolved until commodity dependencies that contribute to the destruction of public forest benefits are scaled back and mechanisms for capturing the diverse values of forest ecosystems are created. *(See Chapter III.)*

Meeting legal and professional responsibilities to sustain diverse forest values will require per-

---

Box 2.7. The "Wise Use" Movement

In 1989, some 20 million viewers watched an Audubon Society television documentary on the logging of old-growth forests in the Pacific Northwest entitled "Rage Over Trees." The program asserted that sawmill owners and the U.S. Forest Service were intent on harvesting all remaining unprotected old-growth forests. Within days of the broadcast, the program was attacked by timber companies, sawmill owners, and timber-industry employees for showing "distorted" images of vast areas of ugly clearcut forests to elicit sympathy for conservation goals. Flooding television stations and advertisers with thousands of letters and telegrams, these groups eventually pressured eight major corporate sponsors of the series to withdraw their support. (Dietrich, 1992)

This coordinated attack was one of the first major victories for the "Wise Use" movement—the latest in a series of pro-development coalitions fighting land-use restrictions. The "Wise Use" movement is a loose-knit collection of perhaps several hundred groups throughout the United States and Canada with a wide variety of interests and supporters—from off-road vehicle enthusiasts and homeowners associations to mining companies and loggers. Disparate as these groups are, they share the belief that private property rights are threatened by government regulation. Some also believe that limits on the use of public lands are unconstitutional.

Some elements of the "Wise Use" movement want mining and logging allowed in National Parks, the Endangered Species and Wilderness Acts dismantled, regulations on wetlands use eased, private access to public resources such as water, minerals, and rangelands expanded but fees kept at far-below market rates, and the unrestricted use of off-road vehicles allowed. Generally speaking, most of these groups want land-owners compensated for economic "damages" caused by environmental regulation and many want fewer restrictions on access and use of publicly owned natural resources.

sonal commitment by forest managers, policy-makers, and the public. Indeed, expanding public and professional awareness of ethical responsibilities to protect forest diversity for future generations may be the most important key to compensating for tenurial systems that don't always balance rights and responsibilities adequately. For example, in 1989, a federal timber-sale planner in the Willamette National Forest in Oregon founded an organization of active and retired Forest Service employees to push for institutional reform, stricter implementation of environmental laws, and a broader definition of forest management. Today, the Association of Forest Service Employees for Environmental Ethics has 11,000 members (approximately 3,000 of them current or retired Forest Service workers). The organization

represents an unprecedented attempt to reform a federal land-management agency from within. (Brown and Harris, 1992)

Notes

1. There is an important but often overlooked distinction between "common property regimes" on the one hand, and "open access" on the other. In a common property regime, a set of clearly defined rights and obligations over a specific area or resource is held by a clearly defined group of users. In an open access situation, neither the rights nor user group is clearly defined, and the situation more or less resembles a "free for all". Confusion between the two has often led to the

---

In the Northwest, where the movement began, timber dominates the "Wise Use" agenda. Many groups have formed in rural communities where local residents feel threatened by attempts to protect old-growth forests and reform forest management. Fighting the reauthorization of the Endangered Species Act, resisting attempts to strengthen state forest practices Acts, and challenging harvest restrictions on public lands in court are at the top of their agenda.

The "Wise Use" movement portrays itself as a grassroots movement. Yet, much of its financing and leadership appears to come from mining and logging corporations, off-road vehicle manufacturers, and from such conservative political groups as the National Rifle Association and Rev. Sun Myung Moon's American Freedom Coalition. Nevertheless, many of these groups have grown rapidly during the last four years among resource-dependent communities without economic alternatives and with no sense that environmentalists and

government are concerned about the community's fate.

The "Wise Use" movement and sustainable forest management seem to be on a collision course. But truly sustainable forest management that addresses the basic economic and social needs of forest communities may eventually diminish the appeal of many of the movement's more ideologically extreme anti-environmental groups. At any rate, proponents of forest policy reform in the United States must recognize what many in tropical countries have learned during the past decade—conservation doesn't stand a chance without sustainable community development. Diversifying local economies and improving access to markets, investing in profitable and sustainable uses of natural resources, and increasing local access to economic and political decision-making processes should be on the agendas of forest policy reformers.

characterizations of common property systems as inherently destructive of the resource base, when in fact many such systems are both sustainable and productive.

2. Government Regulation No. 21/1970 concerning the Right of Forest Exploitation and the Right to Harvest Forest Products.

3. Government Regulation No. 7/1990 concerning the Right of Industrial Timber Plantation Exploitation. Plantations for purposes other than paper-pulp production are limited to 60,000 hectares.

4. If state and private corporations form joint ventures to develop a timber plantation under a HPHTI right, 14 percent of the needed capital can be obtained as a government-held equity investment, taken from the "Reforestation Fund" revenues ($22/cubic meter) levied on extraction of timber from logging concessions, and an additional 32.5 percent can be borrowed interest-free from that source. Where state corporations operate alone, 35 percent of capital costs can be drawn as subsidy from the Reforestation Fund, and an additional 32.5 percent can be borrowed interest-free from that source. The government does not, however, finance the equity of the investor, beyond the interest-free loan. (Joint Decision Letter of the Ministers of Forestry and Finance, No. 421/1990/No. 931/1990)

5. Decision Letter of the Minister of Forestry No. 148/1989 concerning the Rattan Cultivation Right.

6. Decision Letter of the Minister of Forestry No. 208/1989 concerning the Right to Harvest Rattan.

7. Decision Letter of the Minister of Forestry No. 840/1991 concerning the Right of Sago and Nipah Forest Exploitation.

8. Article 6 of Government Regulation No. 21/1970 concerning the Right of Forest Exploitation and the Right to Harvest Forest Products.

9. Indeed, a 1987 study in Irian Jaya province concluded that the process for official registration of *adat* tenurial rights in the central highlands was generally invoked at the instigation of land speculators from outside the community buying lands held under *adat*, as insurance against subsequent claims by other *adat* claimants to the same parcel of land. (Barber and Churchill 1987)

10. Translated by the authors from the original Indonesian.

11. Decision Letter of the Minister of Forestry No. 200/1991 Concerning Guidelines for Formation of Production Forest Utilization Units.

12. Law No. 10 of 1992 concerning Population Development and Family Welfare (unofficial English translation).

13. Some would argue the new approaches are actually a return to older practices such as selective cutting, relying on natural regeneration, etc.

14. The Fifth Amendment of the U.S. Constitution states that no person shall "be deprived of life, liberty, or property, without due process of law; nor shall private property be taken for public use, without just compensation." The Fourteenth Amendment extends due process provisions to state governments: "nor shall any State deprive any person of life, liberty, or property, without due process of law."

15. The federal government does have the power of eminent domain which gives it the right to appropriate private property for public use, with compensation based on "fair" market value to the owner. The exercise of eminent domain is a relatively rare event and most frequently involves land used for transportation and utility corridors where some landowners have refused to sell on a voluntary basis.

16. Which provides the basis for government regulation of activities on private forest lands through state forest practices acts, etc. (*See* Cubbage and Siegal, 1985)

17. The U.S. Forest Service administers 76.4 million hectares, while the remaining 25 million hectares is administered by various agencies including the Bureau of Land Management, National Park Service, and the U.S. Fish and Wildlife Service.

18. This includes 670,000 hectares of forest land on Native American reservations, mostly in eastern Washington.

19. The loss of ownership can take place only through voluntary sale or judicial proceedings involving condemnation for failure to pay taxes or creditors. Involuntary transfers to the government or public utilities under the exercise of eminent domain are relatively rare and owners must be compensated for their losses.

20. Non-owners have extremely limited rights to the direct or indirect use of forest resources on private forest lands, whether for consumptive uses (including the collection of non-timber forest products, hunting, or fishing) or non-consumptive uses (e.g., recreation or free passage). Two major exceptions are that others may own mineral rights to subsurface resources or water rights to water that passes through private forest lands. Non-owners can, however, acquire temporary or limited rights to forest resources through contractual agreements to buy, lease, or exchange ownership rights with the owner.

21. Although the doctrine of waste was used as the basis for some early forest practice laws, the common law of private nuisance is much more often used now as the basis for forest practices legislation.

22. ORS 527.610 to 527.992.

23. "Special resource" sites are determined by the state forester's office and may include sensitive bird nesting or roosting sites, or sensitive habitats for threatened and endangered species.

24. Basically, a private land owner does not have to implement the species-recovery plan unless he or she plans to destroy the habitat of the endangered species in an area where an approved Habitat Conservation Plan (HCP) is in place. The destruction of habitat in areas covered by the HCP requires an "incidental take" permit issued by the U.S. Fish and Wildlife Service. Such permits may require the owner to carry out certain tasks associated with the recovery plan. (Irwin and Wigley, 1992) Certain activities which are listed as threats in the recovery plan could result in prosecution of the forest owner if they do not have an incidental take permit or violate the conditions of the permit.

25. Some argue that private owners would have reforested without regulation because of market forces. Boyd and Hyde (1989) suggest that if this is true, then it is unlikely that state forest practices acts in Oregon and Washington have contributed to net social welfare, unless water quality and other non-timber benefits can be quantified and shown to exceed the cost of administering the law, which in the mid-1980s cost $1.3 million per year ($0.35/hectare). Of course, this makes sense only if one agrees with economists that net social welfare must be defined in economic units that can be easily measured.

26. Rapid urbanization in western Oregon and Washington has swallowed up large areas of private forest lands during the past several decades. In rural areas, many small individually-owned forest parcels (and some commercial timberlands) are being subdivided and developed for vacation homes and other recreational uses often incompatible with forest ecosystem management.

27. Most of this is state land. County governments own 131,000 hectares of timber land in the two states.

28. Washington has much more state forest land (826,000 hectares) than Oregon (308,000 hectares).

29. Virtually all BLM forest lands are located in Oregon, mostly in the southwest part of the state.

30. Most of this forest area is contained in four national parks: North Cascades, Olympic, and

Mt. Rainier in Washington, and Crater Lake in Oregon.

31. Many foresters and forest economists do not feel that timber harvests have been unsustainable despite the large gap between net annual growth and annual harvest levels during the past several decades. The basis for this reasoning is that old growth forests are past optimum rotation age. This happens when the annual growth increment of trees levels off. Trees past this point, such as those commonly found in old-growth stands, are considered to be "overmature." To achieve economically efficient sustainable forest management, it is necessary to replace the old-growth forests (with accumulated high timber volume but low annual growth increment) with younger forests managed on an optimum rotation cycle (where mean annual growth increments are higher, but accumulated volume is lower). According to this view, it is possible to have harvest levels exceeding annual growth rates and still be practicing sustained-yield timber management as long as old-growth forests are being harvested. As the old-growth disappears, there is a "knock-down" to sustained yield levels where average timber harvests equal average net growth levels. One problem with such arguments is that net timber growth figures are based on models that frequently overestimate actual forest growth. The other problem is that moving rapidly to the sustained yield optimum rotation situation will leave some communities with large parts of their surrounding forest area in similar optimum rotation cycles. This means that people (and wildlife) will be subject to a boom and bust logging cycle. To counter this, the U.S. Forest Service for years

managed under a "non-declining even flow" policy that sought to regulate timber harvests such that no annual harvest could be larger than any sustained-yield harvest in the future.

32. Dams, urban development, and pollution have dealt serious blows to natural salmon stocks as well, but most of these threats are found outside of National Forests.

33. The Georgia Pacific Company, for example, recently voluntarily agreed not to log old-growth and mature forest habitat areas of the red-cockaded woodpecker (a threatened species) on its forest lands in the southeastern U.S. In Washington state, Weyerhauser—the largest wood products company in the U.S.—claims to be supportive of the goals of more comprehensive forest practices legislation. (Weyerhauser, 1992) The Plum Creek Timber Company is implementing "New Forestry" principles (meaning they leave about 15 percent of timber volume standing in timber harvest areas as well as leaving dead wood throughout operational areas) on approximately 15 percent of its lands in Washington, Idaho, and Montana.

34. The new rules address the size and timing of harvest units, conservation of critical habitat sites, management of riparian and wetland areas, and the use of chemicals.

35. State forest practices acts, however, have been repeatedly and consistently upheld as constitutional and in the public interest by state and federal courts throughout the United States. (Cubbage, 1991)

III. Economic Development and Forest Utilization

Forest policies and practices have not evolved with perceptions of the forest's true worth. For decades, forests were valued largely for their timber and other commodities, and as a land frontier for crop production and grazing. Today, more emphasis is being placed on the role of forests as a key reservoir of biodiversity, and as important components in the global carbon cycle and hydrological systems, as well as on recreational and aesthetic values. In many countries, the importance of forests as homes to indigenous traditional communities is also receiving increased attention. But these new—or sometimes rediscovered—values are harder to nail down and quantify than the basic commodity values and short-term interests that continue to drive forest policy and management.

As in many other countries, the dominant economic patterns and practices in the forestry sectors of Indonesia and the United States were established in an earlier time on the basis of imperfect information to serve a narrow range of objectives. In both countries, their reappraisal must hinge on consideration of three key sets of economic issues. First, many inevitable shifts in the forest economies of both countries are independent of proposed policy interventions designed to enhance non-timber values. Second, the economic benefits from forest exploitation flow to a limited number of actors, while those who bear the costs are diffuse or are politically marginalized. Third, current and past policies have created strong dependencies on heavy timber harvests, and the resources needed to diversify

timber economies and make them sustainable are large and politically difficult to mobilize.

Underlying these issues is the pervasive misvaluation of forest resources that is built into most countries' forest policy and practice. Consistently, the benefits from intact forests have been undervalued by policy-makers, ensuring that the resource is misused. The net benefits from forest exploitation have been chronically overestimated, while the costs of exploitation have been ignored, and this dual-edged misvaluation has led policy-makers to under-invest in forest conservation and management. (Repetto 1988)

The Economics of Indonesia's Forestry Sector

While Indonesia's forests represent a wide range of values to the nation and its people apart from commodity production—watershed protection, biodiversity, and locally used forest products, to name a few—forest policy and practice mainly serve the interests of large logging and processing companies. This industry has grown explosively in the past 25 years. *(See Box 3.1.)* As of 1991, some 580 logging concessionaires held claim to lands totalling more than 60 million hectares—nearly one third of the nation's land area and more than 41 percent of designated forest lands. (Djamaluddin, 1991) Approximately 25 million hectares of this area had been "logged out" by mid-1990 (WALHI/LBH, 1992), while production continues at over 33 million cubic

Box 3.1. The Explosive Growth of Indonesia's Timber Economy

Although Indonesia now ranks among the largest players in the global timber trade, it did not begin to commercialize its forests until the late 1960s, and the plywood and other processing industries developed only during the 1980s. Before 1967, forest exploitation was confined almost completely to the extraction, processing, and trade of teak from Javanese plantations. Forestry activities outside of Java were small-scale, and nearly all wood was marketed locally. (Departamen Kehutanan, 1986)

The commercialization of Outer Island forests took place as a result of major political changes in Indonesia. In 1966, the military took power, establishing the "New Order" regime that persists today. The new government inherited an almost bankrupt nation saddled with a massive debt, soaring inflation, a stagnant industrial sector, and high unemployment. In this context, forest resources were one of the most liquid assets available for converting to capital and foreign exchange and for improving the balance of payments. By the late 1960s, the legal and institutional structure for the timber-concession system was in place, along with laws facilitating foreign investment, and a timber boom began.

Over the period of the First Five Year Development Plan beginning in 1969, timber earnings rose 2,800 percent, coming mainly from the province of East Kalimantan, where newly-granted logging concessions covered nearly 11 million hectares. (IIED/GOI, 1985) While only four million cubic meters of logs were cut from Indonesian forests in 1967—mostly for domestic uses—by 1977 the total

had risen to approximately 28 million cubic meters, at least 75 percent of that for export. (Barber 1989) Gross foreign-exchange earnings from the forestry sector rose from $6 million in 1966 to more than $564 million in 1974. By 1979, Indonesia was the world's major tropical log producer, with a 41-percent share of the global market and 2.1 billion dollars worth of export value. The country exported a higher volume of tropical hardwoods than all of Africa and Latin America combined. (Gillis, 1988)

Even amid the timber boom, Indonesia's economy remained extremely dependent on sales of oil and gas throughout the 1970s, and oil exports rose from $7.4 billion in 1978/79 to $19 billion in 1981/82. (WALHI/LBH, 1992) By late 1982, however, real oil prices (adjusted for rising import costs) began to plummet, falling by more than 50 percent by the end of 1987. At the same time, prices for rubber, palm oil, tin, and several of the country's other important exports fell. (World Bank, 1988)

To diversify the economy in the wake of this crash, logging quotas were increased, and a major push to "add value" by developing processing industries was launched. In 1982, the government announced a phased ban on the export of unworked logs, and by 1985 the legal export of logs had come to a halt. This policy paved the way for explosive growth in processing facilities after 1985: by late 1988, there were 106 plywood mills in production with a total installed capacity of more than 6.7 million cubic meters per year, and 39 more mills were under construction. (GOI/FAO 1990, Vol. III)

meters annually. Foreign exchange earnings from the export of timber products and rattan totalled $4.2 billion in 1991, more than one fifth of all exports apart from oil. (World Bank 1993) By the

end of the 1980s, Indonesia supplied half of the world's plywood and accounted for more than three fourths of all U.S. imports of hardwood plywood. (Schwarz, 1992a)

Transitions in Indonesia's Timber Economy

In the absence of an accurate forest inventory, or reliable information on actual harvest levels (World Bank 1993), nobody can say with certainty that "Indonesia will be logged-out by year X." On the other hand, by almost any reckoning the country's forestry sector faces a great and rapid transition.

Some simple calculations show that current demand is likely to undermine the forests within a few decades—sooner in some areas. The usual rule of thumb for sustained yield in Indonesia is that one cubic meter per hectare of commercial species can be removed from productive forest annually. (Sedjo, 1987) If this rule and good logging practices were utilized, then supply would be roughly in balance with current demand levels from industry, now and into the future. But, for many reasons, this scenario is unrealistic:

- Much "production forest" is in fact classified as "Limited Production Forest" because of its steep slope, or inaccessibility or other reasons. The level of sustained yield, even under ideal conditions, is thus much lower than 46 million hectares, as claimed after a recent survey. (RePPProt, 1990)

- Collateral damage to standing stock and waste is very high in Indonesian logging operations. For every cubic meter cut, at least an equal amount of usable wood is left behind. (GOI/FAO, 1990, V.2) In all, some 8 million cubic meters are left rotting in the forest annually. (World Bank, 1993) In addition, damage to surrounding trees averages 50 percent, soil compaction impedes regeneration of dipterocarps, and favored species are "creamed" from stands. (Potter, 1991; Brookfield et al., 1990)

- The building of logging roads—and the clearing of areas alongside roads—removes a large area of forest. The 500 km. of logging roads in one large East Kalimantan concession involved "daylighting" clearance of some 40,000 hectares. (Potter, 1991)

- The Indonesian logging system allows a second cut only after 35 years, but no concessions are this old yet, and it is unlikely that they will be able to produce at the levels of the first cut. In neighboring Malaysia, studies theorize, a second cut is possible only if residual stand damage is 30 percent or less, which it isn't in Indonesia. (Thang, 1989)

- According to the Indonesian Forestry Action Programme (GOI, 1991), "a 35-year cycle may be only about half the length of time required to support a sustainable harvest in the long term," though the Programme endorses "continuous monitoring and evaluation" rather than stricter cutting-cycle regulations.

- Few concession-holders properly follow the selective cutting system mandated by their concession agreements, and some observers believe that even a 100-year concession would not provide incentives for better management since concessionaires are simply not interested in a second, less profitable cut that would require years of costly interim management and protection. The possibility of converting "degraded" concessions to timber plantations, with a generous government subsidy, further reduces incentives for long-term natural forest management.

- Logging roads and operations open forest lands to migrant farmers, whose activities make sustained yield—or even maintenance of forest cover—in these areas all but impossible. In 1990, nearly 3 million hectares of production forest and nearly 9 million hectares of "conversion" or unclassified forest were under some kind of agricultural occupation (GOI/FAO, 1990, Vol. 4), and the actual figure may be higher than these estimates.

A 1993 review concluded that an estimated 22 million cubic meters of wood per year could be cut sustainably from Indonesia's tropical forest, but that harvests are currently running 50 percent higher. (World Bank, 1993) In short, natural forests probably can't even slake current demands from Indonesia's wood-processing industries without increased deforestation, much less higher demands over the medium term.

Unlike Thailand and the Philippines, which have exhausted their forests, and Malaysia, where timber extraction looks to be a "sunset industry" under current policies (World Bank, 1991a), Indonesia still has time to reset exploitation targets to reflect ecological carrying capacity and to take the operational realities of timber extraction into account. But a major transition, whether systematic or wrenching, is clearly in store. Recognizing the inevitability of this transition, the government states in its Tropical Forestry Action Programme that "[d]ue to population and industrial growth, the projections suggest that the raw material situation in Indonesia will become critical in about a decade if Indonesia continues to maintain its market dominance and industrial pace, and if forest resource management and utilization efficiency do not significantly improve." (GOI 1991)

The Distribution of Costs and Benefits

Shifting to a sustainable forest economy will require adjusting the current flows of costs and benefits in the forestry sector. As things now stand, relatively few large firms reap the benefits while costs show up as losses of government revenue and losses of livelihood in the communities living off of and near official forest lands.

In timber exploitation, most of the available economic rent—the profits exceeding the minimum that an investor needs to earn to make a given project worthwhile—flows to concession-holders. If calculated on the basis of $145/m^3, which Malaysia realizes on the same or comparable species, available rent per cubic meter comes to approximately $99. The Indonesian government captured only 8 percent of this in 1989 in fees and royalties, while a fee increase in 1990 raised the percentage to 17 percent. In 1993, the government increased royalties by 47 percent to an average of $22 per cubic meter. However, this figure is, according to the World Bank, "still below the $30 level royalties would have reached

by now had they been adjusted from 1985 levels by the wholesale price index for the forestry sector and, hence, is well within the capacity of the industry to pay, particularly considering the recent sharp increases in world log prices." (World Bank 1993) *(See Table 3.1.)*

If the government could capture the 85 percent of rent that it obtains in the oil sector, one study estimates, logging would have contributed nearly $2.5 billion to government revenues in 1990, five times the $416 million actually collected, and more than half of Official Development Assistance received in that year. For perspective, during 1984-1989, total fees and charges levied on forestry operations accounted for no more than 0.2 percent of the government's total domestic revenue and no more than 0.1 percent of the annual government budget. (WALHI, 1991)

Along with low levels of rent capture, artificially low domestic log prices have resulted in "environmental degradation, inefficiency in both logging and wood-processing industries and a lack of market diversification." (World Bank 1993) In 1992, export taxes replaced the ban on log exports, but the impacts on resource use have been negligible because the taxes are high enough to effectively constitute a ban. As a result, while prices for Meranti logs exported from Sabah (Malaysia) have averaged around $160 per cubic meter since 1986, with 1993 prices topping $300, equivalent logs in Indonesia averaged about $90 per cubic meter in 1993—maybe less, since most plywood operations are affiliated with concessions, and thus obtain logs at cost. (World Bank 1993) Another recent study confirmed this analysis:

Several industrialists practicing intra-firm pricing compose a quasi-cartel. Their determination of log prices reflects neither the scarcity value of tropical logs nor the externalities involved in their exploitation. This allows Indonesians to value at only $70–80 per cubic meter the same Bornean species which Malaysians value at $140–165 per m^3. (WALHI/LBH, 1992)

Table 3.1. Calculation of Potential Rent in Timber Production (US $/cubic meter, highly conservative estimate)

	1988	1989	1990
Average FOB Value of Indonesia's Log[a]	145.00	145.00	145.00
Logging Cost[b]	32.00	35.20	38.72
Normal Return to Capital (30%)	9.60	10.56	11.62
Economic rent in stumpage value	103.40	99.24	94.66
Rent captured by government			
Licence Fee, Property Tax & Royalty	4.00	5.00	6.00
Reforestation Fee	4.00	7.00	10.00
Total Rent Captured	8.00	12.00	16.00
Percentage of Total Rent	8%	12%	17%
Unrealized Rent	95.40	87.24	78.66
Percentage of Total Rent	92%	88%	83%

a. The estimated figure is the value of weighted average of log price for logs for plywood and for sawnwood in Sabah port using the log equivalent volume of Indonesia's plywood and sawnwood exports as the weight:

(LESPE*PLP) + (LESSE*PLS) = (0.56*133) + (0.44*160) = US $144.88

LESPE	=	log equivalent share of plywood export
LESSE	=	log equivalent share of sawnwood export
PLP	=	price of log for plywood
PLS	=	price of log for sawnwood

b. Assuming 10% cost inflation per year

Source: From WALHI, 1991.

Although most direct financial benefits have flowed out of the forest areas and into the hands of private concession-holders, it is frequently asserted that considerable indirect benefits accrue to local and provincial economies through direct charges on forestry production, through the "development of backward and remote regions," and through "trickle down" of employment and other benefits to local communities. (GOI/FAO, 1990; Vol. III) But a recent study (WALHI, 1992) on the regional and local economic impacts of the timber industry in East Kalimantan suggests that such benefits are exaggerated. *(See Box 3.2.)*

This large province, which accounts for 10 percent of Indonesia's land area, contains 20 million hectares of legally recognized forest lands. Of this, 12 million hectares is held under 108 timber concessions. From 1980 through 1988, 25 percent of all logs produced in Indonesia came from East Kalimantan, peaking at 30 percent in 1984. Surveying the results of this massive timber boom, the Indonesian Forum on the Environment (WALHI) concluded:

- At current high rates of exploitation and negligible rates of reforestation, commercial

Box 3.2. The Economic Impact of Timber Exploitation on a Village in Kalimantan

The village of Jelmu Sibak lies on the Lawa river in East Kalimantan, within the legally designated territory of two logging concessions. Its 541 residents are mainly indigenous Bentian Dayak people, with a smattering of immigrants from other areas. Most make a subsistence living growing dryland rice and other annual crops, supplemented by fruit trees, rattan, and other forest products. Honey and Gaharu resin is collected, and pigs and deer are hunted. Some villagers keep water buffalo, pigs, and chickens as well. Rice is grown on a rotational basis; particular fields are used for several seasons, then allowed to lie fallow for years until covered with brush and young trees of about 10-20 cm. diameter. Whether in fallow or not, these fields are owned and inherited by particular families. Each family cultivates an average of about 1.7 hectares of rice per year, with a total annual production of about 100 tons, and some plots lie as far as 40 kilometers from the village proper.

After the government banned all traditional logging activities in the early 1970s, and the market for rattan improved, rattan cultivation and collection gradually became the primary source of cash income for the village. Rattan is cultivated in conjunction with both active rice fields and current fallows, but is also sought from former fields of past decades and generations, and from the forest, where animals disperse its seeds.

The village's economy is primarily subsistence, though some products are traded for either cash or goods. Transportation links with larger towns are difficult, whether by river or by logging road.

In 1971 and 1981, two timber concessions that completely encompass the traditional territory and settlement sites of Jelmu Sibak were granted by the government. The local people have continuously attempted to maintain their traditional *adat* rights to their land and resources, but various forestry laws criminalize the long-standing way of life of Jelmu Sibak.

Conflicts first arose in 1982, when the construction of the logging basecamp on *adat* lands destroyed crops, honey trees, and rattan stands and ruined a local cemetery. With support from village and sub-district officials, the logging companies were induced to pay minimal damages—less than 10 cents per square meter for land, 50 cents for a mature fruit tree, and $175 for the ancestral graveyard—and to provide the village with a color television, a satellite dish, and five miles of new road.

In 1989, the two logging companies posted signs on all paths from the village at about 2.5 miles out, prohibiting all farming under penalty of imprisonment and fines up to $50,000, effectively cutting off the villagers from their traditional livelihood and shunting them onto areas too small to support adequate fallow periods. Yields of rice are expected to drop in the next few years.

Logging operations are also directly diminishing the village's harvests of wild rattan, fruits, and other forest products. Meanwhile, the connector road built as the major recompense to the villagers is largely impassable, so the costs of local trade are high.

The logging operations have not created jobs for Jelmu Sibak either. As of January 1992, fewer than ten villagers had even part-time employment with the concessions, and six of those were day laborers. Nor have purchases of village goods by concession employees added up to much. On balance, through logging in Jelmu Sibak, access to the forest's wealth has shifted from the villagers to the concession-holders, damaging the local ecological balance and economic system to the detriment of the local people.

Source: WALHI, 1992

exploitable timber in East Kalimantan will be exhausted by 2003.

- From 1985 through 1990, logging enterprises directly employed only about 2 percent of the population over 10 years of age, while forest industries employed another 4 percent or so.

- Logging and forest industries in 1985 indirectly created an estimated 18 and 45 jobs respectively, per 100 directly created jobs, but these gains are offset by the still-uncalculated but most likely large loss of employment and income from local forest-based cottage industries (e.g., rattan collection) denied access to forest resources controlled by concession-holders.

- Investment in the province's forestry sector is becoming increasingly capital intensive, as shown by the ratio of jobs created per unit of investment (100 million rupiah; $50,000 at 1991 rate) in both logging and forest industries. In logging, per unit jobs declined from nine in the 1970s to six in the late 1980s. In forest industries, per unit job creation declined from eleven to three during the same period.

- From 1975 through 1989, only 28 percent of forestry taxes and levies returned to the province, and only 9 percent of what was returned was used for forestry conservation and development.

- Census data for 1987 through 1990 showed that consumer prices rose more rapidly than the income of the province's poor.

Clearly, appreciable direct and indirect benefits are not reaching either local communities or the provincial government, who are nevertheless paying the costs of the current forestry exploitation system. These costs include loss of all commercially productive forests by 2003, loss of access to non-timber forest products, diminution of hydrological and other ecological functions, and increased risk of forest fires.

Continuing Dependencies on Heavy Timber Harvests

Both forest policy-makers and timber firms can see change in forestry policy and the timber industry coming, and both are aware that Indonesia could run short of raw material for its timber industries in a matter of years. But a powerful industry's dependence on continued heavy harvests narrows the range of options for all.

The log-export ban of the early 1980s and the accompanying requirement that concession-holders develop sawmills and other processing facilities rapidly created a large industry dependent on a continuous supply of timber. Indonesia's plywood and sawn-timber mills need some 44 million cubic meters a year to operate at 80 percent capacity—well above the government-mandated production ceiling of 31 million cubic meters. (Schwarz, 1992c) Either the mills are operating far below capacity, or, more likely, felling far exceeds officially reported levels. (Sedjo, 1987) While the extent of illegal timber removals is by definition elusive, Indonesia's National Police Chief estimates that millions of cubic meters of timber are stolen each year in South and East Kalimantan alone. (*Jakarta Post*, 1993) Even so, many plywood mills are finding it difficult to obtain an adequate supply of logs, especially those in Sumatra and Kalimantan, where forest standing stocks have declined considerably in recent years. Rather than plan for a decrease in the size of the plywood industry to put it in line with sustainable harvest levels, the government is instead urging mills to relocate to Irian Jaya—where the same cycle of exceeding sustainable harvest limits followed by declines in standing stock is likely to be repeated. (*Jakarta Post*, 1993a)

The dilemma is clear: if the country's forests are to be sustained, timber-harvest levels should be promptly halved, and the industry should eliminate the high levels of waste in the plywood production process, estimated to be at least 33 percent (World Bank, 1993) and, in one government estimate, as high as fifty to seventy percent (*Jakarta Post*, 1993a). Yet, the Ministry of Forestry told Parliament in July 1993 that cutting was not keeping up with its annual target of 31.4 million cubic meters and suggested that the industry should raise production to 54.5 million cubic meters annually to feed its processing industries. (Suharyanto, 1993)

The government's strategy for meeting industry's heavy demands rests largely on the ambitious new Industrial Timber Plantation (HTI) program. The new policy framework calls for the development of three types of plantations—mill wood, fuelwood, and pulp/paper/rayon fiber—totalling 6.2 million hectares, but pulp fiber plantations are favored. As of 1992, the Ministry of Forestry had already accepted 353 applications for 12.5 million hectares of plantations (already twice the target for the year 2000), 7 million hectares of that devoted to pulp estates. (WALHI/LBH, 1992) This crash program will help the government make Indonesia into one of the "top ten" pulp and paper producers in the world, but it will also exert new pressures on both natural forests and the people who live in and around them, and it will not reduce wood producers' dependency on natural forests.

What plantations will do is feed a wholly new industry. Investors are likely to site plantations in standing natural forests, not on degraded lands as government would like. A proposal pending in 1991 from the Kian Lestari conglomerate, for example, would involve clear-cutting about 200,000 hectares of natural forests—some currently designated as limited production and protection forests—to make way for fast-growing pulp-stock monocultures. (Dick, 1991)

For several reasons, corporations prefer to site plantations in cleared natural forests. Truly degraded lands, such as those covered with alang-alang (Imperata cylindrica) grass, are difficult to develop into commercially sound plantations. Also, entrepreneurs have the right to clear-cut and sell all natural timber in areas designated for plantation development, and the diversion of the Reforestation Fee—one of several royalties collected from logging concessions—into equity capital and no-interest loans provides a further incentive for plantation development.

What's more, many of the "degraded lands" slated for HTI plantations are useful and productive from a local community's point of view. Secondary forest and scrub areas may be fallows for swidden farming systems, areas for grazing livestock, or sources of fuelwood and other daily supplies. Having lost access to primary natural forests to logging concessions, local communities then find themselves deprived of access to what remains. (See Box 3.3.)

The Economics of the Pacific Northwest Forestry Sector

For nearly 100 years, the Pacific Northwest's economy was dominated by the timber industry. The world's most imposing coniferous forests seemed to promise a never-ending stream of jobs, profits, tax revenues, and building materials. Lumber production was the premier manufacturing industry in the Pacific Northwest between 1880 and the 1970s. West of the Cascades, most rural communities that weren't farming in the Willamette Valley or fishing in Puget Sound were timber towns.

During this era, forests were overwhelmingly valued for their timber. In 1952, the chief silviculturalist for the U.S. Forest Service in the Pacific Northwest called old-growth forests "biological deserts," virtually devoid of life and productivity. (Caufield, 1990) Although prized for tremendous volumes of high-quality timber, every acre of timber slowly wasting away in old-growth forests was also viewed as one less acre of vigorous, highly productive, and biologically healthy forest.

For decades, federal forest policies reflected the "progressive utilitarian" views of Gifford Pinchot (founder of the U.S. Forest Service) and his patron, Theodore Roosevelt.[1] Convinced that the excesses of the timber barons would soon create a timber famine, Pinchot believed forest policy had to ensure a continuous (preferably growing) flow of timber from public and private lands. (Clary, 1986) Conservation meant protecting forests from waste and destruction but not from logging as long as it was conducted to ensure future

Box 3.3. Plantations and People: The Struggle of Sugapa Village

While Indonesian government plans call for a vast expansion of industrial timber estates in the 1990s, particularly to produce pulp, the operations of the Inti Indorayon Utama (IIU) corporation in North Sumatra provide one of the only up-and-running examples of the environmental, economic, and social impacts of timber estate development. As such, it is a cautionary tale.

IIU began operations in 1989 in the region around Lake Toba, the largest lake in Southeast Asia and home to the Batak people. IIU is one of thirty companies owned by the Raja Garuda Mas Group conglomerate. IIU registered profits of $53.6 million in 1989, and Raja Mas plans to expand the Lake Toba operation and to build new plants and plantations in other parts of Sumatra. By the mid-1990s, it will thus become the country's number one paper-and-pulp producer.

IIU gets its raw materials from aging plantation stands of pine (*Pinus merkusii*) dating from the Dutch colonial period, and from its own 150,000-hectare logging concession, parts of which it has clearcut and replanted in Eucalyptus without the appropriate permits. The firm is also cutting forests it owns in the area's crucial water-catchment areas, though these are formally zoned as Protection Forest. As IIU's raw material needs expand, it is seeking new areas to either log or plant in Eucalyptus.

From the start, IIU has locked horns with local communities over a landslide that killed 13 people and forced a whole village to relocate, and over extremely high levels of air and water pollution caused by its operations. Indeed, a massive spill from IIU's waste pond triggered the first environmental lawsuit in Indonesian history—non-governmental groups, which eventually lost the case, charged the company with failure to comply with environmental impact regulations.

Conflicts have also arisen over IIU's restriction of local access to forest lands and resources. Woodcarvers on Lake Toba's Samosir island, for example, are forbidden to collect wood in their own community's forests, and villagers in one area strongly protested IIU's planting of Eucalyptus on their ancestral graveyard.

A particularly divisive conflict erupted in 1987 in Sugapa village when IIU rented 52 hectares of village land for 30 years to plant Eucalyptus. This land was the village commons—utilized for grazing, fuelwood, and gathering berries sold in the local market. The villagers did not recognize the land transfer since it violated the local customary tenure system. For the loss of this land—and thus of their ability to raise water buffalo—the village was paid only $6.35 per hectare, less a $5 charge every time a buffalo wandered back into its pasture. Eventually, the villagers were forced to sell their herds—a great loss considering that families kept five to ten buffaloes, selling one a year for $400–600.

After the villagers protested to the company, several village men were harassed and beaten. In April 1989, when two plantation workers were accused of trying to rape a village girl, the villagers decided to act, ripping up 16,600 Eucalyptus seedlings the company had planted. Police arrived and alerted the company, but arrested only the ten women involved, not the workers accused of rape. Since local customary law places land ownership in the hands of male heads of households, the women could thus not be said to be defending their property. Riding roughshod over customary law in acquiring the land, the company later used it in support of the criminal charges for property destruction brought against the ten women, who were sentenced to six months in jail for destroying property and "obstructing national development."

(continued on next page)

The women appealed, and the appellate court offered to excuse them from jail if they would promise to commit no further "criminal acts." Maintaining that they had never committed a crime, the women rejected the court's decision and appealed to the National Supreme Court, which had not rendered a decision as of mid-1993. Angered by this result, several other villagers brought a civil suit against IIU and the local government for abuse of customary tenurial rules and procedures. IIU offered to settle the case by paying rent for the land, but the many villagers who do not want a plantation under any conditions are harassed continuously by local officials. Meanwhile, the case has split the formerly harmonious village into three hostile factions—those for, against, and undecided on the rental offer.

In at least eight other villages, IIU has similarly taken advantage of weak documentation of ancestral community land rights, and

government, IIU, and the courts have conspired to intimidate and even prohibit local non-governmental organizations (NGOs) from helping them. One local NGO that had been advising the Sugapa villagers was shut down without explanation by the government for six months, and allowed to reopen only on the condition that it stop dispensing legal aid.

Annual per capita income in Indonesia	$495
Market Price of one 3-year old buffalo raised in Sugapa	$500
IIU's compensation for taking land for 30 years, per ha	$6
Charge each time one buffalo enters former pasture	$5
Compensation villagers seek from IIU	$30,000
IIU's annual profit	$53,600,000

Source: (WALHI/LBH, 1992)

undiminished harvests. Dissenters included such wilderness advocates as John Muir and those in the timber industry who categorically opposed any forest policy.

In recent decades, new knowledge and increasing scarcity have changed the values attached to natural forest ecosystems, especially to old-growth forests. The consensus around Pinchot's vision of forest policy began to erode in the 1960s, as the public became more interested in the non-timber benefits of forests. Today, the biodiversity, hydrological, recreational, and climatic values of forests are more appreciated than ever before.

But while the "new values" are of growing importance to an increasingly (sub)urbanized country, rural economies largely dependent on timber values persist, as do the relatively narrow economic interests of commodity-based corporations that control much of the access and rights to forest resources. This concentrated dependence on commodities has frustrated attempts throughout

the United States to make forest policy and management better reflect the changing mix of values attached to forests by the general public. In the Pacific Northwest, the struggle over the fate of the remaining old-growth forests outside of National Parks and legally protected wilderness areas has intensified during the past decade, becoming perhaps the most visible manifestation of the clash over which forest uses and values to emphasize in public policy.

In other parts of the country, the transition to forest policies that sustain a wide array of forest values is no less difficult. But below-cost timber sales, marginal physical and economic forestry conditions, and clearly undervalued recreation and environmental assets all convincingly argue for forest policy reform. *(See Box 3.4.)* Indeed, some sort of reform seems imminent. Shortly after taking office, the Clinton Administration proposed eliminating below-cost timber sales as part of its deficit-reduction plan. Although the administration dropped the original proposal

Box 3.4. Below-Cost Timber Sales On Public Lands

In March 1993, the U.S. Forest Service released its annual accounting of National Forest timber sales from the previous year. Although the agency concluded that 68 of 122 national forests lost money, the timber sale program overall earned $256 million in 1992. (USDA, 1993a) A couple of months later, the Cascade Holistic Economic Consultants (CHEC) released its own analysis, indicating that the Forest Service timber program lost $453 million. (O'Toole, 1993) This was the latest in a long series of disagreements—by now an annual spring ritual—between the Forest Service and critics of its timber sales program. Below-cost timber sales (i.e., those in which the costs of producing timber and administering sales exceed receipts) have become a focal point for advocates of U.S. Forest Service reform.

Differences between Forest Service estimates of net timber sale revenues and those of many analysts (e.g., O'Toole, 1993; Repetto, 1988; Beuter, 1985; GAO, 1984; Wolf, 1984; Sample, 1984) inside and outside of government generally come down to what costs should be counted against timber receipts. The Forest Service counts two categories of costs—timber sale expenses and timber program expenses—against annual timber revenues. Timber sale expenses include administrative costs, such as conducting timber surveys in sale areas, advertising and conducting sales, monitoring harvest operations, etc. The timber program costs include long term-capital expenses—those associated with road surfacing, culvert construction and maintenance, reforestation and timber improvement, etc.—amortized over an extended period and charged against timber sales during that period.

Forest Service accounting, however, departs from standard accounting practices in curious ways. For example, past expenses (e.g., the amortized reforestation costs) are not accumulated with interest while future benefits (e.g., future timber harvests in reforested areas) are not discounted back to a common base year. (Repetto, 1988) Moreover, the agency often amortizes reforestation costs over periods much longer than a typical rotation and road construction costs are often amortized beyond their average life expectancy. Beyond that, the agency charges only some road-construction costs (surfaces, bridges, and culverts) against the timber program, ignoring most road construction costs (for the base layer of the road or the "prism") altogether. (O'Toole, 1991) The Forest Service justifies this as a capitalized land improvement—not a cost—even though the National Forests already have a 370,000 mile road network and the agency spent $90 million decommissioning roads in 1992. The benefits of new roads are questionable given the well-documented costs existing roads already impose on increasingly valuable non-timber resources. Finally, as critics point out, county payments from timber sales should be treated as costs (the Forest Service likes to think of them as revenues) since they are payments in lieu of taxes that private owners must pay.

Although various independent analyses (e.g., O'Toole, 1993; Repetto, 1988; Beuter, 1985; Sample, 1984; GAO, 1984) define costs somewhat differently, their conclusions are remarkably consistent. First, timber sales on National Forests in the Rocky Mountain states, in Alaska, and in the East are chronically below-cost. Second, most U.S. Forest Service acreage managed for timber production produces taxpayers losses that exceed the profits made in the Pacific Northwest and a handful of National Forests elsewhere in the country. Over the past decade, these analyses show, overall losses to the Treasury total between $200 and over $500 million annually, depending on the cost criteria used and the year.

(continued on next page)

The Forest Service recognizes that below-cost sales do occur, but argues that timber management activities yield closely-linked costs and benefits (joint benefits and costs) that produce net social goods. Roads built for logging trucks can also be used by recreational vehicles, and logging increases forage for elk and other wildlife. Such benefits and costs, however, are extremely difficult to measure and allocate. Meanwhile, most evidence suggests that the agency overestimates non-timber benefits from logging and underestimates the costs. Perhaps more important, the supposed beneficiaries of the joint benefits, including state Fish and Game agencies, conservation groups, and outdoor recreational users, frequently oppose Forest Service logging plans. (Repetto, 1988)

Below-cost timber sales have come under increasing scrutiny in Washington in recent years as policy-makers have become more concerned about timber-related losses to the Treasury and environmental damage in areas economically and physically unsuited to timber production. That they have survived testifies to the difficulty of reforming even the most obviously flawed forest policies.

under political pressure,[2] the Chief of the U.S. Forest Service announced in April 1993 that the agency plans to end logging in 62 National Forests (none of them in the Pacific Northwest) plagued by below-cost sales. (Schneider, 1993)

In the Northwest, highly productive forest lands and high prices for valuable old-growth timber have made heavy harvesting economically attractive to the timber industry, even without the government subsidies so prevalent elsewhere. In addition to the misvaluation of forest resources, three major features of the Northwest forest economy contribute to policy-makers' reluctance to embrace forest policy reforms. First, technological change, shifts in timber-industry investment, and log exports all take a toll on the timber-based economy by eliminating jobs and potential revenues. Second, the principal economic benefits of heavy harvests go to a comparatively small group while the costs are generally spread around. Finally, past forest policies have created century-old economic dependencies on high timber-harvest levels and left communities with few economic alternatives.

The Changing Timber Economy

The domination of regional and local economies by timber in the Northwest is coming to an inevitable close. What was once a large forest economy fueled by a voracious appetite for old-growth timber is rapidly becoming a smaller forest economy supported by less valuable second-growth timber. Along with the rapid liquidation of old-growth trees, the transition to a smaller forest economy in the Northwest is driven by improvements in labor and technological productivity and by relatively high production costs compared to other regions.[3] (Sample and LeMaster, 1992) At the same time, the regional economy has diversified dramatically as service and professional industries have grown in urban areas, further shrinking the comparative role of the timber industry.

Despite record cutting levels during most of the past decade, the timber industry lost at least 10,000 jobs between 1980 and 1990. (Haynes, 1992) All segments of the forest industry together now employ about 4 percent of the total work force in Oregon and Washington, still higher than the national average, but much lower than levels of ten and twenty years ago. Increasing automation and other productivity improvements in the forest industry have reduced labor requirements from an average of five workers per million board feet of processed lumber in 1980 to only four workers in 1990[4] (Sample and LeMaster, 1992), and the newest mills require only about

1.75 workers per million board feet. (Flora, 1990) This trend is predicted to continue during the next decade (Sessions, et al., 1990),[5] though the job losses may be less rapid than during the 1980s since most surviving mills will have already invested in labor-saving technologies.

Increases in log exports from private and state lands have also put a damper on processing activity and pushed employment downward in the Pacific Northwest.[6] Between 1963 and 1988, log exports from Oregon and Washington increased by nearly 500 percent (Flora et al., 1991), averaging 3.1 billion board feet between 1984 and 1988. (Adams and Haynes, 1990) This volume is equivalent to over half of the total sawtimber harvest on forest industry lands in western Oregon and Washington and over one quarter of all timber harvested in the region in the late 1980s. Assuming that four jobs are created for every million board feet milled into lumber, these exports potentially cost 12,000 timber industry jobs (and an additional 15,000 to 27,000 indirect and induced jobs) during the 1980s.

Of course, timber exports create jobs as well—as many as 5,800 jobs in Oregon and Washington. (Flora 1990) If log exports were banned, only a fraction of these export jobs would remain, (those serving the needs of offshore log buyers who decide to substitute finished lumber products for at least some raw logs). Other buyers will no doubt shop for logs in other countries (e.g., Russia) instead. (Flora, 1990) Some experts argue that further export restrictions would end the U.S. "monopoly" on supplying high-grade softwood logs,[7] sacrificing lucrative markets and government tax revenues on log sales.[8] (Sedjo et. al., 1992, Flora and McGinnis, 1989) In any case, log exports hit domestic mills and their workers particularly hard— the same businesses and people who would bear most of the brunt of forest policy reforms.

The past decade has also seen a dramatic shift in forest industry capacity from the Pacific Northwest to the southeastern United States. During the 1960s, the Pacific Northwest had 37 percent of all U.S. lumber and plywood capacity, compared to 23 percent in the South. By the mid-1980s, 40 percent of lumber and plywood capacity was in the South, and capacity in the Northwest had declined to 30 percent. (Adams, et al., 1987) This shift mainly reflects higher delivered log costs in the Northwest, where harvesting is more expensive due to steeper terrain and the use of more complicated and capital-intensive logging systems.[9] Technological advances also allow the forest industry to use the lower-quality southern pines in an ever wider variety of products. And, with rotation times for loblolly and other southern pines typically ranging between 25 and 35 years, compared to 45 to 75 years for Douglas fir in the Northwest, industry investment in the South is more profitable.

Protection of endangered species and policies to lower timber harvest levels will visit additional burdens on some timber-dependent communities. Already victims of a large-scale transition they cannot control, forest industry workers, representatives of forest industries, and local communities fiercely oppose forest policy reforms. Trying to offset losses from the larger economic transition transforming the regional timber economy, these interests seek to prolong logging in old-growth forests and other forest areas where intensive timber management and the sustainability of non-timber benefits are increasingly incompatible.

Concentrated Benefits and Diffuse Costs

The benefits of high timber harvest levels, of course, have also come at considerable cost. But the nature of the costs is in many ways different from the nature of the benefits. Few people can attribute lost jobs to the disappearance of an old-growth forest in the same way that a logger or a mill worker might if the forest was protected. Many of these costs are hidden or at least difficult to measure, and logging is often but one of several factors degrading the forest and related resources.[10] Although it seems safe to say that depleting mature timber stocks and liquidating old-growth forests will generate severe long-term opportunity costs, the short-term costs—geographically and economically diffuse—are more difficult to enumerate than the benefits. Federal and state policy-makers have thus been naturally reluctant to embrace forest-policy reforms.

The principal beneficiaries of timber-driven forest policies have been the forest products industries, their employees, and the communities that house them. Wages in the timber industry in Washington and Oregon contributed $2.5 billion to the economies of those two states in 1988. (U.S. Department of Commerce, 1992) In some counties, especially west of the Cascades, timber industry and related indirect and induced employment provide more than 25 percent of all jobs. Many of these counties also benefited from over $500 million in local government tax revenues[11] generated by timber-industry activities on private and public forest lands in Oregon and Washington. And, despite complaints about environmental restrictions on logging, some segments of the timber industry (especially large integrated firms) with extensive operations and landholdings in the Northwest reported record or near-record production levels and profits for lumber and plywood in 1992 in their annual reports.[12]

Nevertheless, recreation, biodiversity, conservation, fisheries, and other forest resources are increasingly competing with timber as valued forest uses in the Pacific Northwest. Tourism and recreation is a huge business in the region, contributing more than $6 billion annually to the economies of Oregon and Washington in the mid-1980s. (Wilderness Society, 1988) Wildlife-related recreation[13] in Oregon and Washington alone totals at least $2 billion annually. (USFWS, 1988) Nationwide, National Forests get over 280 million visitor days for recreational use (USDA, 1992), more than ten times the use in 1950. (Repetto, 1988) National Forests in Oregon and Washington alone enjoyed 44 million visitor days in 1991.[14] Conservatively assuming that 25 percent of all wildlife-associated recreation reported by the U.S. Fish and Wildlife Service took place in the National Forests, the value of expenditures related to hunting, fishing, birdwatching and other non-consumptive wildlife recreation in these forests may have totaled over $500 million in Washington and Oregon in 1985 (USFWS, 1988), or about two-thirds the value of National Forest timber sales in 1988. Were they

marketed, O'Toole (1988) estimates, recreational and other "amenity benefits" (such as fish and wildlife) in National Forests in the Northwest would be worth approximately one third as much as timber values.[15] Currently, the U.S. Forest Service collects only about 2 percent of the estimated value of recreation benefits. (O'Toole, 1988)

Salmon and other anadromous fisheries[16] are also a major economic activity often in conflict with forest policies in the Northwest. In 1989, these fisheries were valued at approximately $150 million in Washington and Oregon. (U.S. Department of Commerce, 1992) According to U.S. Forest Service estimates, the commercial value of salmon and steelhead produced in streams in the National Forests of California, Oregon, and Washington totals $120 million. (USDA, 1987) The fisheries industry employed at least 13,000 in the Northwest in the late 1980s. (U.S. Department of Commerce, 1992)

Policies encouraging high timber-harvest levels have been undercutting the potential of both fisheries and the tourism/recreation industries. In the Suislaw National Forest in Oregon's Coast Range, clearcuts and logging road construction account for more than 75 percent of the landslides that have blocked streams or otherwise damaged habitat and spawning grounds for coho and chinook salmon and sea-run cutthroat and steelhead trout. (Anderson and Gehrke, 1988) Commercial and sport fisheries catches have remained relatively stable during the past decade (Washington State Office of Financial Management, 1992) only because hatchery-planted fish are growing in number. Throughout the region, natural fish stocks are in serious trouble: most remaining natural runs of anadromous fish are considered to be at moderate to high risk of extinction during the next century unless expansive and costly restoration efforts are undertaken. (Thomas et al., 1993) Although demand for roadless recreation in Oregon's and Washington's National Forests is projected to increase dramatically in coming decades, plans for individual National Forests completed in the 1980s indicate that their capacity to meet this demand would drop between 40 and 75 percent on some National Forests if roadless areas were opened for logging as planned. (Wilderness Society, 1988)

The costs of losing recreational opportunities would hit far more people than the benefits of heavy timber harvests, but the impacts would be diffuse. The outdoors-lovers who seek natural forest environments come from a heterogenous population throughout the region, the country, and the world. For the most part, the tourism/recreation industry also serves a large clientele interested in many attractions besides natural forests. And the fisheries industry, relatively small compared to the forest-products industry anyway, has many employees who work outside the industry for much of the year.

The benefits of protecting watersheds and biodiversity are also diffuse and difficult to quantify. Potential beneficiaries include such disparate groups as makers and users of the new anti-cancer drug taxol,[17] mushroom hunters and restaurants, and landowners in flood plains. In the Northwest, thousands of people are affected each year by flooding and landslides linked to or exacerbated by extensive clearcuts in steep watersheds above. While disaster victims may be hardest hit, taxpayers end up paying more for road and bridge repairs. In other cases, ecologically unsound logging practices contribute (along with heavy rainfall and snowmelt) to flooding, making it difficult to apportion blame and costs.

A clean environment, recreational opportunities, and other components of "quality of life" have been at least partially responsible for the growth of some of the region's most important economic sectors. A high quality environment influences investment decisions and job growth in high technology, professional services, and other high-value economic sectors. But as Rivlin (1993) points out, the political decision process emphasizes benefits that can be measured, appropriated, and valued in monetary terms—so many board feet of timber sold, for example. On the other hand, the process tends to neglect diffused social benefits—clean air, wildlife habitat—that cannot be easily measured despite their apparent value to society.

Dependencies and Transition

A regional economic transition away from natural resource-based sectors to a more diversified economy based on trade and services has already been taking place in Washington and Oregon. During the 1980s alone, while jobs were lost in the forest industry due to mechanization and the export of more raw and fewer processed logs, trade added 126,000 jobs to the economy and the service sector grew by 246,000. (Northwest Policy Center, 1992)

New forest policies that protect old-growth forests and give increased emphasis to non-timber values will add momentum to the shift—at least in the short-term. To ease this transition, the region needs alternative employment, education and training, investment capital, government revenues, and established markets for more sustainably produced timber and non-timber forest resources.

Occupational and Cultural Shifts in Logging Communities Jobs lost in logging and timber manufacturing will have to be replaced by employment in other occupations. In the Northwest, unemployed timber workers and job openings do not make a perfect match. Most new employment is in urban areas in the professional, service, and trade sectors while rural employment in manufacturing is declining. In Oregon and Washington, the fastest growing economic sectors include restaurants, medical and health services, food stores, business services, social services, and professional services. (Sommers, 1988) Employment in heavy construction—where unemployed loggers might be able to use acquired skills—isn't growing. Without additional education or training, most forestry-industry employees cannot enter professional jobs, and wages in basic service industries (restaurants, tourism) are usually a fraction of those in the timber industry. As William Dietrich notes in *The Final Forest: The Last Great Trees of the Pacific Northwest*, part of the tragedy of the economic demise of rural timber towns in this region is that they represent the end of an era in which blue-collar America could live in beautiful affordable places with comparatively high-paying jobs.

In any case, for many in the forest industry, adaptation to long-term social and economic change is painful. Like family farming, logging represents a way of life, not simply a way to earn a living. Getting trees out of the woods is a strenuous and dangerous occupation that most loggers consider more rewarding and more valuable than virtually anything else they could do. (Carroll, 1989) But loggers may be clinging to cultural and social beliefs at odds with the technological revolution of the past half century. According to Carroll (1989), "Strongly developed occupational role identities which motivated loggers to the dirty and dangerous work of their occupation appear to be a hindrance to successful adaptation to a changing economy. If successful change is to occur, the logger's social organization must adapt to economic changes exogenous to his immediate world. The outcome is uncertain, and the stakes, from the logger's point of view, are very high."

Workers intent on staying in the forest industry will be hard-pressed to find work outside the region as well. Workforce reductions notwithstanding, the forest industry in Oregon and Washington remains an important regional employer relative to its size in most areas in the United States. In 1990, it[18] employed 137,000 people in a regional workforce of nearly 3.25 million. (Washington State Employment Security, 1992b; Sessions et al., 1990) This accounted for almost 20 percent of all manufacturing jobs.[19] In contrast, the timber industry at the national level employs only 4 percent of all U.S. workers in manufacturing. (U.S. Department of Commerce, 1991) *(See Box 3.5.)*

For some rural counties in the Pacific Northwest, employment in the forest industry is much more pronounced and supports a high percentage of jobs and income.[20] In the twelve rural nonmetropolitan Washington counties west of the Cascades,[21] on average 12.5 percent of all jobs (and over 60 percent of manufacturing jobs) are in the forest industry. These jobs generated over $636 million in monthly wages—nearly a fourth of all wages paid in the twelve counties. *(See Table 3.2.)* In rural southwestern Oregon, between 20 and 30 percent of all jobs are in the timber industry. (Sessions, et al., 1990)

The economic impact of the forest industry goes beyond what these direct employment figures suggest. Sample and LeMaster (1992) estimate that for each job in the forest industry, another job is indirectly supported or induced by service demands from the industry and spending generated by its workers. According to this rule of thumb, in seven rural Washington counties west of the Cascades, between 26 and 50 percent or more of all jobs come from the forest industry directly or indirectly.

At the same time, these counties have had unemployment levels substantially above the state average in 1992. (Washington Employment Security, 1992b) When timber harvests on federal lands were greatly reduced in 1991, following court orders to protect the northern spotted owl's habitat, unemployment levels in the counties most dependent on federal timber increased.[22] In Skamania County, Washington, where 27 percent of all employment is in the forest industry and nearly 90 percent of the sawtimber volume is on Forest Service lands, unemployment rose from 15.5 percent in March 1990, before federal timber sales were judicially restricted in May 1991, to 32.6 percent in January 1993. (Washington Employment Security, 1993; 1992b) Already struggling with high unemployment rates and the timber industry's reduction in force, communities like these will take any further loss of jobs in the forest industry as a bitter blow.

Government Revenues Government will play an important role in the transition to more sustainable forest economies. But to help those affected by the transition, it must raise additional revenues to meet increased demand for the public services needed to buffer economic and social changes. They will also have to find a substitute for declining federal timber receipts. For perspective here, U.S. Forest Service timber sales in 1988 totaled nearly $881 million in Washington and Oregon (Ulrich, 1990)—25 percent of which went directly to county governments.

Government financing is essential for funding job training and education programs and for providing career counseling and social services in

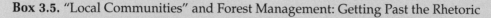

Box 3.5. "Local Communities" and Forest Management: Getting Past the Rhetoric

Many of the tensions and conflicts that stymie forest policy changes in both Indonesia and the United States revolve around differing views about how much authority and control local communities should have over forest resources. In this often pitched battle, environmental advocates are sometimes accused of inconsistency in their treatment of local communities and their proper roles in forest policy-making and forest management. When greater community control augurs well for conservation, the argument goes, environmentalists back it. But when a local community favors commercial exploitation of forests at the expense of some environmental value, then environmentalists advocate stronger governmental controls in the interests of "broader societal interests."

In all cases, strengthening local management is desirable, and giving communities incentives to manage natural assets sustainably should be a primary goal of forest policy. Yet, environmentalists and policy-makers must respect each community's unique economic and social structure, as well as its historical relationship to forest lands and resources. Wise policy is flexible enough to take all such differences into account and adjust accordingly.

Even communities found within a particular region—be it Oregon or South Sumatra—are of many different kinds, and governments—or environmentalists—have no right or way to categorize communities as "good" or "bad" stewards and managers. Still, some variables typically distinguish different kinds of communities and thus provide some basis for predicting their potential for safeguarding the forests' productivity and diversity:

1. Is the community's relationship to the forest multifaceted? Communities with diverse, multiple ties to the forest are more likely to value the long-term integrity of the whole ecosystem than those whose relationship is restricted to one or two narrow objectives, such as timber extraction or mining.

In Indonesia's Irian Jaya province, for example, forests provide wood, game, fruit and other foods, craft materials, and medicines for many communities. They regulate the water supply and figure in the community's religious life. In some communities in Sumatra's Kerinci Valley region, on the other hand, the forest is largely viewed as a "resource" to be cleared and replaced with lucrative cash-crop mono-cultures of *Cassiavera* (cinnamon) trees. Communities in both areas have a long history on the lands in question, and both have legitimate interests in influencing decisions about how forests in their areas are used. But, it would be naive to think that "handing over" the forests to the cinnamon farmers of Kerinci would lead to anything (apart from high short-term profits for some) other than rapid forest degradation, increased erosion, biodiversity loss, and deforestation in the region.

In the United States, some forest communities in northern California, the Rocky Mountain states, and northern New England among other places are trading one monolithic relationship with the surrounding forest (i.e., intensive logging) for another (i.e., recreational development and subdivisions). In either case, forest fragmentation, biodiversity loss, and declining water quality are side effects. But in other communities around the country, diverse community interests are now negotiating compromises to protect the sustainability of surrounding forest resources. In Mendocino County, California, such discussions led to a package of measures to slow forest fragmentation, establish systems of long-term ownership management plans, rebuild forest stock, and restrict activities detrimental to riparian, watershed, and wildlife habitat quality.[1] (Romm, 1993) In the Applegate

(continued on next page)

57

Valley of southwestern Oregon, diverse stakeholders are cooperating to develop broadbased forest management plans and incentives to sustain public and private forest resources. Such transformations occur only where access to economic and policy decision-making processes controlled principally by outside government and corporate interests is opened to the community at large. (Honadle, 1993; Rivlin, 1993; Romm, 1993)

2. Are the community's economic relationships to the forest direct or mediated by outside organizations? In some communities, local individuals or institutions directly manage economic relationships with the forest. Examples include subsistence relationships, such as hunting for game that is directly consumed, or small- to medium-scale market activities, such as a local sawmill that draws logs from forests in the immediate area. In other cases, a community's economic relationship is not so much with the forest as it is with an intermediary organization from outside of the community, such as a large commercial firm or development project.

Not every community with direct economic relationships with the forest will manage it sustainably—witness the cinnamon farmers noted above. But most such communities have the capacity to change their management approach if they choose or can be persuaded to do so. In contrast, a community working through an intermediary—say an externally-based logging firm—can't easily change the firm's relationship to the forest.

3. Do members of the community, or the community as a whole, possess long-term tenurial rights over forests lands in their area? Where a community's members own local forest lands and resources, they tend to take care of them over time. Where they do not own land, but rather, have an interest in, say, the wages generated by logging, their stake in the overall long-term health of the forest won't be as great.

4. To what extent do community members share a common history, culture, and local social organization that could control forest access and other management functions? Some communities have more social cohesion and ability to control their members and outsiders than others, and such cohesion can grow or disintegrate. ("Community" becomes a uselessly vague concept, for example, when applied equally to a newly established Indonesian logging camp and a traditional clan of forest-dwellers.) Some communities in the U.S. Pacific Northwest began as helter skelter logging camps but have evolved into effective functional communities. Where members of a settlement have not developed—or have lost—the ability to reason together from a common cultural basis and to take effective collective action to direct and control human activities, how can it be expected to take on an active role in sustainable forest management?

The degree of community management and control needed to support forests' sustainability into the next century will always lie between the poles of giving communities complete control to do whatever they wish and allowing government agencies and large commercial firms to dictate forest uses strictly for their own purposes. Striking the right balance for a particular forest area and its communities will depend in large part on whether policymakers, environmentalists, and local communities themselves, can get beyond rhetoric and begin to ask questions such as those posed above.

---

1. The negotiations were carried out by a committee appointed by the county board of supervisors. Unfortunately, industrial forestry members of the committee withdrew their support for the recommendations at the end of the process. Romm suggests this may have happened because the county and state did not do enough to legitimize the trades made within the negotiating framework of the committee. (Romm, 1993)

Table 3.2. Washington Forest Industry Employment and Income Patterns in 1990.

Location	Forest Industry Employment	% Manufacturing Employment	% Total Employment	% Total Wages	Jan. 1993 % Unemployment
Statewide	60,007	16.3	2.8	3.6	9.1
Metropolitan Counties	31,130	10.7	1.9	2.3	7.4
Rural Counties W. Cascades	20,570	63.4	12.5	23.0	13.6
Skamania	513	94.0	27.6	30.7	32.6
Cowlitz	7,354	72.0	21.6	32.6	12.5
Grays Harbor	4,039	72.2	18.0	25.9	19.0
Mason	1,707	82.1	17.5	25.8	11.8
Wahkiakum	100	77.5	15.5	26.4	16.0
Lewis	2,908	68.6	13.8	17.6	14.6
Clallam	2,248	81.0	13.0	30.0	12.3
Pacific	647	44.0	11.4	20.0	15.7
Skagit	866	22.1	2.8	5.5	14.5
Jefferson	90	11.5	1.8	2.3	10.9
San Juan	53	22.3	1.4	1.0	10.8
Island	35	7.7	0.0	0.1	7.2

Source: Washington State Employment Security (1993, 1992a, 1992b).

timber towns. Government can also provide low-interest loans and other financial support (lower tax rates, tax credits, infrastructure development, purchases of goods and services, and short-term subsidies) to encourage individuals to invest in new businesses and economic activities—whether furniture production from underutilized tree species or tourism and recreation. Since private investment capital for small enterprise is scarce in rural areas, government backing for private-sector investments may be crucial to the survival of many timber-dependent communities, especially those that have relied on old-growth timber supplies from public lands.[23]

Unfortunately, the timing is bad. Both Washington and Oregon have seen growing state government budget deficits in recent years. In the most recent biennial budget period, Washington state government deficits increased to nearly $1.2 billion, compared to a total budget of roughly $30 billion. (Washington Office of Financial Management, 1991) Oregon, with a $7.5 billion state budget in 1992, had a deficit of nearly $500 million. If these deficits continue as expected, state legislators will be under increasing pressure to trim spending.

County governments, especially those in timber-producing areas, may face even greater financial problems. Although county finances in Washington and Oregon have been generally sound, their financial health has benefited from the 25 percent of the gross receipts they receive from timber sales on National Forest lands in the county, and in 18 Oregon counties from the 50-percent share of gross timber sale revenues from Bureau of Land Management (BLM) lands. (Lee et al., 1991) In 1988, sales from the National Forests brought in $220 million in revenues for 25

Oregon and 18 Washington county governments. In Oregon, ten counties depend on federal timber revenues for between 25 and 66 percent of their income. *(See Table 3.3.)* In western Oregon, federal timber receipts from both the National Forests and BLM lands totaled $235 million in 1990 (Lee et al., 1991), or 22 percent of all county government expenditures.[24] Local governments also enjoy revenue from taxes paid by timber industries and from severance taxes paid by private timber owners. (Sessions, et al., 1990)

Lowering harvest levels could reduce county revenues substantially unless property taxes increase or other revenue sources are found. According to Lee et al. (1991), implementing plans to protect the northern spotted owl could reduce county revenues by an average of 23 percent in timber-producing counties west of the Cascades. If so, cut-backs in public health services, law enforcement, and social services would come at the same time local governments are grappling with unemployment and economic dislocation.

The federal government, itself deficit-ridden, may be reluctant to increase or alter discretionary funding of any kind. Already, federal revenue-sharing programs that could compensate local governments for lost timber revenues have been dramatically cut during the past decade.

Timber Supply Although second-growth timber has become increasingly important to the timber industry, not all firms can use these slimmer trees. Many sawmills produce premium grade products that can be manufactured only from the huge logs found mainly on public lands. In 1987, some 22 percent of sawmill capacity in western Washington and Oregon was totally dependent on old-growth and large sawtimber supplies. (Olson, 1988) An additional 45 percent of sawmill capacity was partially dependent on old-growth. In the wake of the 1991 court injunction, that figure is undoubtedly lower, but opponents of forest policy reform continue to make an issue of this dependence.

Another way to gauge the dependence of sawmills on public timber is to look at their land holdings. Firms without land depend on public timber since private supplies are more expensive when they can be found at all.[25] West of the

Table 3.3. County Government Dependency on Federal Forest Receipts, Western Oregon, 1990.

	Total Expenditures	Federal Forest Receipts	Federal Forest Receipts as % of County Expenditures
Curry	$15,848,935	$10,432,503	66%
Douglas	78,258,931	50,365,813	64%
Josephine	30,528,076	16,757,416	55%
Klamath	38,263,665	19,412,306	51%
Jackson	49,780,189	23,716,089	48%
Linn	36,278,086	14,399,104	40%
Lane	141,716,019	51,366,375	36%
Coos	24,735,992	8,143,322	33%
Tillamook	13,785,286	3,604,932	26%
Columbia	9,233,057	2,264,169	25%
TOTAL	424,346,236	200,462,029	47%

Source: Adapted from Lee et al. (1991)

Cascades, up to 35 percent of the sawmill capacity belongs to landless firms. (Olson, 1988) These mills will be hard hit by old-growth protection and other reforms that reduce the public land harvest unless new policy breaks help them make the switch to second-growth timber. Then too, many smaller companies lack the capital needed to invest in new efficient milling technologies that would enable them to process smaller logs profitably.

Some Washington counties are particularly dependent on sawtimber from National Forest timberlands. *(See Table 3.4.)* In several western counties, at least 30 percent of the sawtimber volume comes from National Forest lands, and the figure is generally higher in eastern counties. Similar patterns exist in Oregon. Considering that three quarters of forest-industry sawtimber is less than 50 years old (Adams and Haynes, 1990)—too young to harvest—actual dependency on federal timber may be even more pronounced in some areas.

The current entrenched local political opposition to forest policy reforms targeted at public lands is only natural. Forest policy reform efforts

Table 3.4. Washington Sawtimber Volume by Timberland Ownership

Location	Total Volume (million board feet)	National Forests	Percent Sawtimber Volume Other Public	Forest Industry	Other Private
Statewide	239,989	37.2	24.3	23.8	14.7
West	168,660	35.4	21.0	28.0	15.6
East	71,239	41.5	31.9	14.0	12.6
Western Counties With highest volumes (57 percent of volume west of Cascades)					
Skamania	21,987	86.7	7.2	3.0	3.1
Grays Harbor	18,600	12.7	19.1	52.7	15.5
Lewis	19,409	46.3	12.8	27.5	13.4
Snohomish	13,703	46.7	20.4	15.1	17.7
Clallam	11,193	36.9	31.4	22.0	9.7
Skagit	11,129	41.3	27.4	18.8	12.5
Eastern Counties With highest volumes (79 percent of volume east of Cascades)					
Okanogan	12,742	41.5	45.7	3.9	8.9
Yakima	11,057	37.1	56.5	5.3	1.1
Ferry	8,542	33.6	52.8	5.1	8.5
Stevens	8,248	18.5	32.5	17.5	31.5
Kittitas	8,014	52.3	9.0	34.0	4.7
Chelan	7,840	77.0	4.3	12.2	6.5

Source: MacLean et al. (1992); Bassett and Oswald (1983)

now focus on public forests, and nearly all reforms would result in substantially lower harvests. At present, timber industries and workers remain skeptical of the local economic benefits a broader, more sustainable forest economy would provide.

Consumer Preferences Adopting more sustainable forest-management policies and practices will probably raise consumer prices for wood products and perhaps for recreation and many other non-timber forest resources as well. Consumers have enjoyed low prices for wood products[26] because harvests are heavy and prices do not reflect the costs that such harvest levels impose on other parts of the economy and on the environment. As a result, the consumption of wood products from lumber to paper continues at levels that are unsustainable: many resources found in Northwest forests—from salmon and clean water to non-consumptive recreational pursuits and biodiversity—simply can't last at today's use rates. Market demand for sustainably produced wood products could become an important incentive for reforming forest management in many parts of the world (Johnson and Cabarle, 1993), including the Pacific Northwest. Although various programs to certify sustainably produced wood products are emerging in the United States, consumers currently have scant opportunity to "vote with their pocket books." Moreover, it is unclear whether the market for such products is large enough to influence producers.

Toward Sustainable and Equitable Forest Economies

Four key conclusions arise from this analysis of the forest economies of Indonesia and the United States. The first is that most of the profound changes that forest economies are experiencing are not affected one way or another by policy interventions intended to conserve forest resources and ecological services. In the U.S. Pacific Northwest, overharvesting, technological changes, increasing production capacity in the southern United States, and large increases in log exports account for the forest industry's declining importance. In Indonesia, the transition is less far along, but just as inevitable: timber production from natural forests is headed toward exhaustion if current logging rates and practices are maintained. Absent policy changes, the likely fate of Indonesia's forests and forestry sector can be seen in the mirror of neighboring Thailand, which has become a timber importer, the Philippines, which has devastated almost all of its forests, and of Sabah and Sarawak (Malaysian Borneo), where commercial timber will be exhausted in the coming decade or so at current cutting rates (World Bank 1991).

However inevitable these transitions, forest policy will influence the nature, speed, and costs of transition, as well as the distribution of those costs. If the growing consensus in favor of increased protection of "new" values in the forest—such as biodiversity, the rights of forest-dwelling communities, or the protection of hydrological functions—solidifies, transition costs will undoubtedly increase, and the burden of these costs may hit some actors or communities particularly hard. Saving endangered species and threatened ecosystems requires immediate steps to protect forest systems, such as the old growth of the U.S. Northwest and the remaining lowland rainforests of Sumatra and Kalimantan, but such action will cost some timber-dependent communities and industries jobs and revenues. To ensure that the benefits and burdens of an unstoppable transition are equitably shared is the only recourse.

Second, economic policies past and present have made many towns and counties dependent on unsustainably heavy timber harvests. In Indonesia, a large forest-products industry created by policy interventions in the 1980s has come to depend on cheap timber supplies, in part to capitalize timber firms' diversification into other sectors; and the sheer size, concentration, and profitability of this vertically-integrated industry has made it a powerful political player in blocking policy change. In the United States, some rural areas, particularly in the Pacific Northwest, depend on logging and the forest industry for over a third of all employment and over half of all local government revenues. The economic survival of many small landless firms depends on the availability of large sawlogs from public forests. Meanwhile, larger firms with their own timberlands exported their own logs profitably and used the relatively cheaper public timber supplies to prolong the profitable life of aging processing facilities that are increasingly uncompetitive with forestry-investment opportunities in the South. As a result, political pressures to maintain high harvest volumes and to resist forest-management reforms are intense.

Third, those who have reaped the economic benefits of forest exploitation have not paid the attendant costs. In the United States, logging practices have been linked to significant losses in fisheries production, water quality, and recreational opportunities—losses that virtually everyone absorbs. But a few Americans (salmon fishermen, among them), pay dearly, and the timber industry pays none of these costs. So far, biodiversity losses due to forest mis-management in the Pacific Northwest are probably low, but an increasing number of species will face extinction in the coming decades as natural forest habitats disappear. Others will diminish in number. Logging has contributed significantly to the decline of salmon, trout, sturgeon, and other fisheries, causing millions of dollars in annual economic losses. It could also wipe out the Pacific Yew (the source of the life-saving drug Taxol) and other still-undiscovered pharmaceuticals.

Meanwhile in Indonesia, the uncounted costs of logging—such as erosion of the resource base for millions of forest-dependent rural people, the loss of biodiversity, and the degradation of water supplies and systems—have been visited on communities in or near production forests, on public agencies that must pay for erosion control and other losses of ecological function, and on citizens at large, who are rapidly losing the economic benefits of the country's great biological wealth.

Finally, formal and *de facto* systems of collecting economic rent from logging and forest industries are extremely inefficient, allowing the private sector to reap excessive profits at the expense of the public treasury. In Indonesia, estimates of uncollected economic rent on forest exploitation in the late 1980s range from 70 to 83 percent, and only a small proportion of the rent collected through government fees and royalties is reinvested in sustaining the natural forests.

In the United States, actual and potential rents are more closely aligned, but timber extraction on federal lands is highly subsidized in other ways. The costs of timber management and timber-sale preparation exceed sale revenues in six of eight National Forest regions. Moreover, many of these below-cost timber sales take place in environmentally sensitive areas where lasting environmental damage is the typical legacy. In the Northwest, timber sales generate large revenue surpluses for the U.S. Forest Service, but the agency subsidizes private timber harvesting by paying for road construction and reforestation. As for other forest resources, such as recreation, the Forest Service captures only a minute fraction of potential economic rents.

Unless these four structural issues are squarely addressed, neither the United States nor Indonesia is likely to enter the coming century with a healthy and productive forest estate that provides the broad range of goods and services both societies now require. Nor will the costs and benefits of forest management and exploitation be equitably distributed. If either country is to make sustainable forestry a reality, significant policy changes will be necessary, beginning with the reform of policy-making itself.

Notes

1. Roosevelt stated that the goal of forest policy was "not to preserve the forests because they are beautiful, though that is good, nor because they are refuges for the wild creatures of the wilderness, although that, too, is good in itself; but the primary object of our forest policy…is the making of prosperous homes… A forest which contributes nothing to the wealth, progress, or safety of the country is of no interest to the government and should be of little interest to the forester."

Theodore Roosevelt address ("Forestry and Foresters") to the Society of American Foresters, March 26, 1903, as quoted in Clary (1986).

2. A half dozen senators from western states objected that the proposal put an undue burden on their states and threatened to withhold support from the administration's economic plan. Clinton withdrew the proposal from the economic program and promised to pursue the end of below-cost sales separately (which environmentalists charged would never get past timber industry lobbyists and western senators).

3. These lower-cost production areas are mainly in the southern U.S. and Canada.

4. Olson (1988) cites a 13 percent decrease in direct timber industry employment in Oregon and Washington between 1980 and 1986 while output climbed to record levels, based on data from the U.S. Department of Commerce, Oregon State Department of Human Resources, and Washington State Department of Employment Security.

5. Compared to late 1980s timber industry employment, Sessions et al. (1990) forecast a loss of 6,200 timber industry jobs in Oregon by 1995 even without increased environmental protection. Approximately 40 percent of the job loss is due to technological change and 60 percent due to a return to sustained-yield harvest levels (harvests during the late 1980s were above sustained-yield levels). However, an increase in finished wood products manufacturing (e.g., cabinet making, moulding and millwork, etc.) is forecast to increase by 2,000 jobs, resulting in a 4,200 net job loss in the forestry sector by 1995.

6. Log exports from federal lands were prohibited in 1969, and log exports from Washington state lands ended in 1992. A long-standing log export embargo from Oregon state lands was renewed in a voter referendum in 1989 by a 9:1 margin. (Flora, 1990) All log exports from Oregon and Washington now come from private lands.

7. Most other countries that are exporters of softwood, such as Canada, restrict log exports or are small exporters in comparison to the United States.

8. The loss of federal tax revenue may not be a good argument for maintaining log exports, however, since log exporters receive generous tax credits estimated at $100 million annually for exports to foreign subsidiaries according to several members of Congress (including Representatives Kotpetski and Wyden of Oregon, and Senator Baucus of Montana) who introduced legislation in 1993 to eliminate the tax breaks or switch the tax breaks to support reforestation rather than log exports.

9. Although labor costs in the Northwest are about 25 percent higher than in the South, higher productivity levels in the Northwest mean that labor costs are competitive with those in the South.

10. For example, salmon runs have been adversely affected by the construction of roads, dams, irrigation canals, and urban development in addition to the impacts directly caused by logging operations.

11. Including real and personal property taxes paid by the timber industries, severance taxes paid by private timber owners, and revenue shares from timber harvested on U.S. Forest Service, BLM, state forest, and county forest lands.

12. These corporations included Weyerhauser, Georgia Pacific, Champion, Louisiana Pacific, and Willamette Industries.

13. Wildlife-related recreation includes hunting, fishing, and non-consumptive activities such as birdwatching and wildlife photography.

14. Of which approximately 20 percent was for hunting, fishing, hiking, and various forms of non-consumptive fish and wildlife viewing activities. The other 80 percent included camping and picnicking in developed sites, skiing, motorized travel sightseeing, and visits to resorts, cabins, and organized camps. Many of these visitors, of course, also participated in recreational activities that are closely associated with diverse natural forest ecosystems.

15. In other parts of the country, recreation benefits exceed timber benefits, by nearly three to one in some Rocky Mountain areas, and they exceed timber values when the aggregate values for national forest resources are compared. (O'Toole, 1988)

16. Fish, such as salmon and steelhead trout, that spawn in freshwater rivers and streams and migrate to the ocean for the adult phase of their life cycle.

17. Taxol is a compound extracted from the bark of the Pacific yew, a small tree associated with late successional and old growth forests in the Pacific Northwest. Taxol is proving effective against breast, ovarian, and possibly other cancers. Yet the Pacific Yew was for decades treated as a "weed tree" that was piled and burned following logging in late successional forests. Although chemical synthesis is likely within the next year or two (and cultivated Pacific Yew became available in commercial quantities in mid-1993), those depending on taxol have thus far had to rely on supplies found in late successional forests.

18. Forest industry employment here refers to jobs in forestry, lumber and wood products manufacturing, and in pulp and paper manufacturing.

19. Based on Washington labor statistics, (Washington State Employment Security, 1992a), most forest industry jobs in the region are in lumber and wood products manufacturing (46 percent), and pulp and paper products manufacturing (30 percent). The remaining jobs are in logging (16 percent), and nurseries, reforestation, and forest management (4 percent).

20. Even within some urban and suburban counties, the timber industry is much more important than it is on a regional basis. In Clark County, Washington (Vancouver, WA), forest industry employment accounts for 6.5 percent of all jobs, and 30 percent of manufacturing sector jobs.

21. These counties include: Clallam, Cowlitz, Grays Harbor, Island, Jefferson, Lewis, Mason, Pacific, San Juan, Skagit, Skamania, and Wahkiakum.

22. Sample and LeMaster (1992) have analyzed several studies (Anderson and Olson, 1991; Gordon et al., 1991; USDA, 1991; Beuter, 1990) forecasting job losses due to old-growth forest conservation. The estimates in these studies range between 15,000 and over 100,000 jobs, most of the difference being due to the use of different multiplier factors for indirect and induced employment that depends on direct timber industry employment. After reconciling assumptions underlying the estimates, they show that the four studies indicate a decline in timber-related employment of between 19,000 and 34,000 between 1990 and 2001. Harvest levels on federal lands may fall by 30 to 40 percent during that same period due to restricted old-growth harvests.

23. Although there is considerable evidence to suggest these functions are best left to the private sector, or government-private sector partnerships. *See* Chapter V for further discussion.

24. It should, however, be noted that county government dependencies on federal timber revenues may not be as prominent as they appear. For example, average per capita county government expenditures in counties with large federal timber revenues in some cases (e.g., Curry and Douglas counties) are double the U.S. average per capita county expenditures (U.S. Department of Commerce, 1992). Moreover, as income from timber declines, counties will receive federal payments in lieu of taxes (PILT) determined by a standard formula if PILT payments are greater than timber receipts.

25. Mainly because owners of private timber can sell their supplies on the lucrative international log market, which gives them higher returns than the domestic market where large supplies of public timber (that can't be exported) depress prices.

26. Seasonal prices do fluctuate dramatically, and there has been upward pressure on wood prices in 1993, which many analysts blame on the timber stalemate in the Pacific Northwest.

IV. The Political Economy of Forest Policy Reform

Two questions must be answered to determine what the underlying problems with forest policy-making are and how to fix them. First, who benefits from which current forest policies and how? Second, what structural and functional aspects of forest policy-making give some stakeholders undue influence, perpetuate unfounded assumptions underlying forest policies, and inhibit change?

Answers to these questions differ in Indonesia and the United States, since the two cultures have different forest policy-making processes that pose different obstacles to policy reform. But an overriding parallel is striking: in both countries, the forest policy-making process itself stands in the way of reform.

Forest Policy-making in Indonesia

Like the rest of the government, Indonesia's forestry agency is highly centralized, reflecting the historical struggle of successive regimes to build and maintain a cohesive nation out of a far-flung archipelago with hundreds of distinct cultural groups and languages, as well as numerous religious traditions. The Ministry of Forestry, its regional offices, provincial forestry services, and the four state-owned forestry corporations together employed about 47,000 people in 1989—3,700 in Ministry headquarters, 29,000 at the provincial level, and 14,000 in the four state enterprises (upwards of 12,000 just at the State Forestry Corporation that manages Java's

forests.) More than 200,000 people work in private forestry enterprises. (GOI/FAO, 1990 Vol. IV) Within the Forestry Ministry, the Directorate General for Forest Utilization is the most influential office, with jurisdiction over logging concessions and forest industries activities and revenues. Numerous regional offices reporting directly to the Minister represent the Ministry in the provinces, and the four parastatal corporations are also basically under the Ministry's control. *(See Figure 4.1.)*

Three elements influence how the forestry bureaucracy makes policy: the nature and functions of law in Indonesia; conflicting bureaucratic management styles; and the prevailing norms, assumptions, and priorities of the forestry professionals who staff that bureaucracy.

The Indonesian Constitution grants control of forest lands and resources to the state, which the current government interprets as exclusive authority over all aspects of human activity within any territories classified as state forest lands. "The Rule of Law," heralded by the government as the ultimate justification of its political authority, and as the governing principle of public life, means orderly obedience to the state, whose power flows both from the Constitution and from *Pancasila*, Indonesia's official five-point state ideology. In theory, laws and regulations are certain in meaning and form part of a coherent whole that orders the state apparatus itself, social organization and action, and the relationship between state and society. But Indonesian law also wears

Figure 4.1. Indonesian Ministry of Forestry

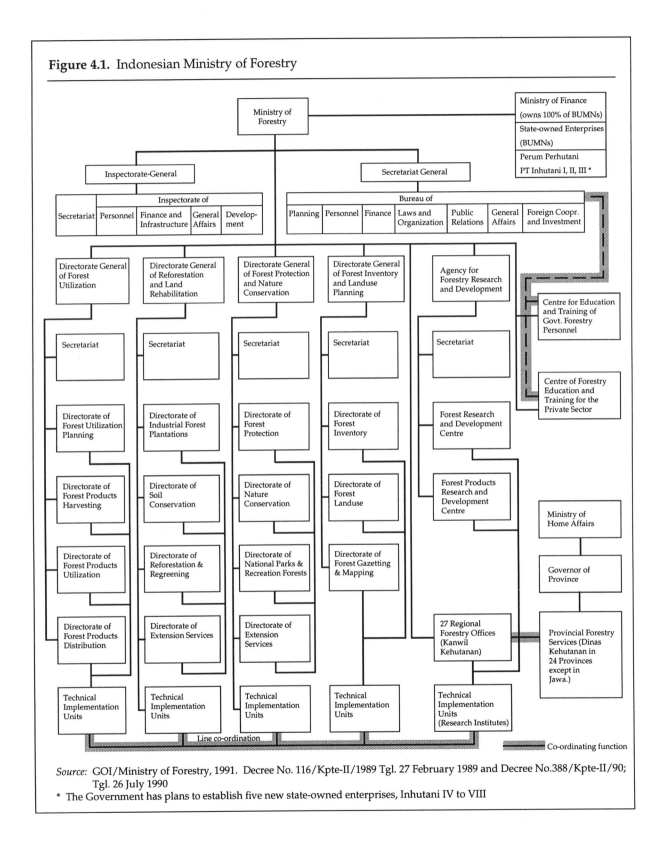

Source: GOI/Ministry of Forestry, 1991. Decree No. 116/Kpte-II/1989 Tgl. 27 February 1989 and Decree No.388/Kpte-II/90;
Tgl. 26 July 1990
* The Government has plans to establish five new state-owned enterprises, Inhutani IV to VIII

another face—the empirical reality of law-as-rules, a complex, overlapping, and constantly changing body of laws, decrees, and administrative regulations that are often applied erratically. Forests and forest policy are thus governed by both an unassailable core of exclusive and comprehensive authority held by the state, and a vast body of indeterminate and often-contradictory laws and regulations that delegate *de facto* authority over many aspects of forest policy and management to the private sector, while effectively abdicating authority altogether in other respects.

At the same time, the Indonesian bureaucracy vacillates between following a rational bureaucratic management ideal and operating through personalized "patron-client" relationships. Under the bureaucratic ideal, a formal hierarchy coordinates action for specific purposes, law is central to the system, and experts make, interpret, and carry out laws and regulations within a clearly defined mandate. In practice, the bureaucracy does not live up to this ideal, though it does powerfully influence assumptions and discourse related to how forest policies are and should be made.

The numerous forestry sector reviews and action plans produced in recent years (e.g., GOI, 1991; GOI/FAO, 1990) describe the bureaucratic ideal and merely hint at day-to-day realities and the bureaucratic undertow of "patron-client" authority relationships,

> …a system of relatively autonomous, highly personal groupings, bound together by a diffuse sense of personal reciprocity found between patron and client. Each group or circle is composed of a set of unequal but reciprocal obligations between leaders and followers… These diffuse, personal, face-to-face enduring noncontractual relationships are the primary social cement integrating Indonesian organizations to the limited degree that they are integrated at all. (Jackson, 1978)

These relationships function within the vast and complex structure of forestry laws and regulations and are shaped by it. The formal rules and regulations are by no means a facade, but on the other hand, many important deals and decisions are made in the back room. The ideal bureaucracy is thus constantly at odds with the patron-client system, and each influences the other.

The third key element in forest policy-making, besides law and bureaucracy, is the "corporate culture" of Indonesian foresters and forestry institutions, a culture characterized by:

- A highly centralized, pyramidal hierarchy and process for making decisions about projects and expenditures;

- Strong reliance on traditionally trained professional foresters in top management positions;

- A close relationship between the forestry service and large-scale user industries;

- An urban and upper-middle class bias among policy-level foresters;

- A strong colonial forestry tradition and background;

- Patterns of forestry sector development assistance that are technically based and executed in cooperation with the forestry bureaucracy and that tend to reinforce existing structures and ways of doing things (Douglas, 1985); and

- The belief that good forest management means creating legally-gazetted forest reserves managed by a professional forestry service comitted to multiple-use, sustained-yield practices that balance demands for industrial timber production with the maintenance of basic environmental services.

- The concomitant belief that the land-use practices of local people usually obstruct these objectives, forcing the forest service into a territorial or custodial role in limiting local access and use. (Wiersum, 1987)

In the field, the formal vision and structures of state-led forest management run up against serious limitations and contradictions. First, the legal mandate of the Ministry dwarfs its capacity to manage, or even monitor, forestry. There is only one professional staff per 127,100 hectares of production and protection forest, for example, and one per 111,000 hectares of park and reserve forest, in the forests, except on Java. In East Kalimantan, the ratio of staff to hectares of production and protection forests is 1:314,000. (GOI/FAO, 1990, Vol. IV)

Second, the large body of forestry laws and regulations are complex and, in some cases, self-contradictory, but there is no formal process for appealing a bureaucratic decision and obtaining an authoritative interpretation that is binding on the bureaucracy. Third, government policies assume that public officials hold sway over forest management, but most officially-recognized personnel in the forestry sector work for private firms, and the millions of local people who practice forest management on a daily basis go unrecognized—or are condemned as interlopers—in the official policy environment. Fourth, Forestry Ministry policy relies heavily on technical approaches to silviculture and criminal-law approaches to enforcement, but the conflicts between local people living in and around forests and agents of government policies are not easily amenable to either approach.

Resolving these contradictions will require significant policy changes accompanied by changes in the processes and institutions that set policy priorities and make decisions. In this respect, the challenges therefore range beyond the forestry sector *per se* to cross-cutting issues of public participation, institutional accountability, and other general issues of public administration.

Who are the Dominant Stakeholders?

The three major groups of stakeholders who benefit most from Indonesia's current forest policies are also the key players in forest policy-making. First, the commercial firms that dominate timber production and processing have reaped immense benefits from current policies. Second,

"bureaucratic capitalists" (Shin 1989) within government form mutually beneficial business relationships with private firms in the forestry sector. Third, members of the state forestry bureaucracy itself have authority over nearly three quarters of the nation's land area.

The benefits that a relatively limited number of private enterprises receive from the forest policy as currently structured are enormous, as discussed in Chapter III. Private profits are huge, and any incentives for efficient wood use undermined. (World Bank, 1993) Lifting export restrictions and increasing rent capture could, the World Bank estimates, generate up to $2 billion a year in additional forestry fees. (Schwarz, 1992a) Ostensibly, something approximating that sum is currently accruing to private firms.

In Indonesia, close links between political and economic power have characterized economic development for 25 years. Forestry revenues have been both a major source of hard currency for the state treasury from the late 1960s on, and major sources of financing for political and military elites. Hundreds of concessions (HPHs) appeared in the late 1960s, many linked to various military organizations, including three regional military commands in Kalimantan. (Shin, 1989) A 1971 study (Manning, 1971) noted that over one million hectares of concession area had been given to five paramilitary organizations, representing 10 percent of the total forest area set aside for production and 20 percent of that in production at the time. Numerous concession-holders also clustered around other centers of power in government. Unlike private businesses that simply have good political connections, many of these companies were bureaucratic capitalists, not serving the interests of individual capitalists so much as "provid[ing] collective benefits for the political figure of the state institution with which it is associated." (Shin, 1989)

After the logging and log-export boom ended in the early 1980s, the prevalence of bureaucratic capitalist enterprises declined somewhat in the forestry sector, though the importance of political-economic relationships did not. Today, many powerful civilian or military political figures, or their family members, are partners, silent or otherwise, in ventures with the country's large business conglomerates. According to a 1990 survey on the timber industry, about 25 "timber kings" in effect controlled the country's forestry sector. In 1988, aggregate sales by the ten largest of these conglomerates exceeded $1.5 billion, mostly from timber-related businesses. (*Warta Ekonomi*, 1990) A number of these same conglomerates are expected to dominate the expanding pulp and paper industry soon too. (Friedland, 1991) *(See Box 4.1.)*

According to the *Far Eastern Economic Review*, Indonesia's most visible and outspoken "timber king" and chair of both the umbrella trade association of forestry producers and various chambers that set policy for plywood companies, sawn-timber mills, and producers of rattan and other forest products—"is unquestionably the strongest player in setting Indonesia's forest policies…" While forestry policy is nominally under the direction of the Ministry of Forestry, trade associations such as Apkindo [the plywood group headed by this timber baron, Bob Hasan] and individual businessmen have enormous influence. Apkindo, for example, tells mill-owners how much they will produce, where they will export, and at what price. (Schwarz, 1992b; 1992c)

Important stakeholders with a lower profile than the timber conglomerates are the nearly 50,000 members of the forestry bureaucracy itself. Their jobs and power both depend on the Forestry Ministry retaining sole legal authority over most of the nation's territory. In addition, it is widely believed—though difficult to document beyond a few well-publicized cases—that some officials collect various unofficial fees, kickbacks, and shares in businesses from concession-holders, contractors, and others who require official action of some kind to pursue their businesses. (Clad, 1991; Shin, 1989)

While it might be expected that local communities would support the forest policy *status quo* if many jobs are at stake, as they have in the United States, this is not the case in Indonesia, where contracted labor has been drawn from geographically

dispersed areas, timber-extraction activities have in many places restricted net income and employment opportunities for local communities by cutting off access to a range of forest products, and independent labor activity is generally discouraged by the government. (Aznam, 1992) Accordingly, timber industry spokespersons—not workers—raise the issue of "jobs" in defense of existing policies, and the details of wages and working conditions in logging and forest industries are not part of the public policy debate.

Neither the businessmen nor the forestry officials who benefit from current forest policy arrangements have much personal incentive to worry about who gets hurt by these policies and how. Since both groups are urban, erosion, landslides, decline in rural water supply and quality, or loss of direct access to forest products does not affect them immediately. Some businessmen do not even worry much about exhausting Indonesia's timber since they are part of conglomerates diversified into many industries. And many forestry officials aren't overly concerned either because Indonesia's plans to develop industrial timber plantations and pulp-and-paper industries in the next several decades include them.

That said, many in government and the private sector are concerned about the declining state of Indonesia's forests and the social inequities and conflicts that current policies are bringing about. With the blessing of international and national environmental groups and of international donors facing their own environmental lobbies at home, the Ministry of State for Environment and the National Development Planning Board consider current forestry policies environmentally unsustainable and believe they will entrain dire consequences in the medium term if not revised. Economists in the Ministry of Finance—supported by the World Bank—believe that current policies allow the private sector to collect too much economic rent from the forests, at the expense of the government—a belief some domestic environmental non-governmental groups share. (WALHI, 1991) Progressive private forestry firms—some motivated by international pressures to halt rainforest destruction—have also

Box 4.1. Prajogo Pangestu, Indonesia's Largest Timber Operator

Prajogo Pangestu, president of Indonesia's Barito Pacific Group, reportedly controls more of the world's tropical rainforests than any other individual. Barito holds concession rights over 5.5 million hectares across Indonesia and has built the world's largest plywood operation, with exports of $2.5 billion between 1987 and 1991. Reliable financial information on the ten companies that make up Barito's wood empire is hard to obtain, but *The Far Eastern Economic Review* estimates the total value of the concessions and associated wood-production facilities at $5 billion to $6 billion.

Born the son of a rubber farmer in Kalimantan, Prajogo rose quickly during the "cowboy" days of Kalimantan's timber boom in the 1970s, when he forged financial relationships with Japanese companies to create the Djajanti Group, then the country's largest timber company. In 1976, he obtained a small concession on his own and parlayed his Japanese connections into capital and logging equipment. When the prospect of Indonesia's 1980 log

export ban sent raw wood prices into a tailspin, Prajogo bought more than 400,000 hectares of concessions from financially distressed companies. With the continuing help of his Japanese partners, Prajogo built dozens of plywood factories, further expanded his concession holdings, and diversified into sugar and oil-palm plantations, banking, real estate, and petrochemicals. Prajogo's plans for the 1990s include a $1.8-billion plant to manufacture olefins (the precursor materials for plastic) and a $1.2-billion pulp-and-paper facility complete with a 300,000-hectare timber estate.

Prajogo translated his vast holdings into considerable clout in forest policy-making. While most other prominent Indonesian businessmen have used their political connections to amass wealth, Prajogo "was a capitalist before he was a crony," according to a fellow businessman. Apart from the contributions that Prajogo makes to national development plans by virtue of being one of the biggest employers in rural Indonesia—he is also believed to be

made a long-term commitment to maintaining the country's natural production forests through innovative management.

Sustainable forestry also finds advocates among strategic thinkers in government and the military who worry about the potential for social unrest as public distaste for the great concentrations of wealth held by the forestry conglomerates grows, along with conflict over the use of forest lands by expanding forest industries. This group also rightly fears ethnic tensions: eight of the ten largest forestry sector conglomerates are headed by ethnic Chinese magnates—frequent targets of popular resentment and occasional attacks throughout Indonesia.[1]

Although these four groups are growing and their agendas for forest policy reform are converging, a serious high-level debate on alternative visions and models for the country's forests has barely begun. The two-year process leading to the promulgation of the Indonesian Forestry Action Programme (IFAP) (GOI, 1991) was dominated by debates over what forestry projects to propose to international donors (and which parts of the bureaucracy would control them). Only minor and marginal changes in the existing system were debated. At the February 1992 Roundtable meeting on the IFAP, one forestry official surprised the assembled donors, policy-makers, and NGOs with the comment that "this is not the place to discuss forestry policy." (Barber, 1992) one of two businessmen who covered Bank Duta's 1990–91 loss of $420 million in foreign exchange.

A March 8, 1991 memo obtained by the *Far Eastern Economic Review* provides a rare insight into how those at the top of Indonesia's timber industry influence policy decisions. The memo, from Prajogo to President Suharto, asks for assistance in getting the Minister of Forestry to speed up paperwork and financing for the industrial timber estate that will supply the $1.2-billion pulp-and-paper mill mentioned above. On the memo, the President wrote to the Minister that he should fulfill all of Prajogo's requests and told the Minister to contact the Transmigration Minister to recruit emigrants from Java for the project. By May 1991, Prajogo had received a license for a 500,000-hectare timber estate in a joint venture with a state-chartered forestry company—becoming the number one company in timber plantations overnight—and plans to obtain financing for the mill complex were proceeding smoothly.

Despite such high-level backing, Prajogo ran afoul of the Ministry of Forestry in July 1991, when the Minister fined Barito Pacific over $5 million for logging violations on a Kalimantan concession. Barito refused to pay, however, and the Ministry dropped the matter.

In 1993, Prajogo took Barito Pacific Timber public on the Jakarta Stock exchange, overnight becoming its single largest component at 12 percent of the Exchange's index weighting. While a coalition of Indonesian and overseas environmental groups began a campaign to urge investors not to buy the company's stock, the lure of the earnings that the world's largest integrated plywood company is able to make in Indonesia's timber economy was enough to ensure that the stock issue was rapidly oversubscribed. In response to environmentalists' protests, Prajogo told *Indonesian Business Weekly* that "They talk nonsense. Their actions are irresponsible."

Sources: Indonesian Business Weekly 1993; Schwarz and Friedland, 1992.

In this setting, innovation is difficult, and only those with specialized knowledge or political relationships have any real power. Until the laws governing forestry are simplified and rationalized, full public participation becomes the norm, and mistaken ideas about forest management are ferreted out of government—all through open public debate—it will be difficult to bring about the substantive policy reforms that could set Indonesian forest policy on a more sustainable footing. *(See Box 4.2.)*

Public Participation and Access to Information

Apart from weaknesses in the legal and regulatory system, the norms and mechanisms governing public participation also hinder change in Indonesia's forest policy-making system. Both the direct participation of local communities in policy and project decisions that affect their vicinities and the participation of non-governmental organizations (NGOs) in policy dialogues and decisions at the central and provincial levels of government are inadequate.

In general, Jakarta policy-makers view rural communities and societies as relatively backward and ignorant—ripe for a state-led transformation into more modern, technologically- and market-oriented patterns of agriculture, settlement, social organization, and industry. This development program reflects government's desire to increase

The Constitution of 1945, Indonesia's supreme source of law, can be implemented in three ways: by Decree of the People's Consultative Assembly, by Statute, and by Presidential Decision. Statutes, such as the Basic Forestry Law of 1967, are implemented through government regulations signed by the President and promulgated by the State Secretariat. Below the government regulations are the ministerial decisions [*Surat Keputusan Menteri*–SK] implementing provisions for higher orders of law and regulation. An article in a Statute or Government Regulation may, for example, establish a general principle or policy, but delegate the promulgation of implementing regulations to a Minister, whose Ministry then drafts a detailed SK. Ministers can also issue SKs on their own, by virtue of their responsibility for running the Ministry. In turn, a Ministerial SK may delegate specific regulatory authority to the Minister's Director Generals, who then issue their own SKs—typically, detailed documents on the procedures and internal administrative requirements for carrying out one regulation or another.

Within the Ministry, draft SKs are usually prepared by technical staff with help from the relevant Directorate General's Legal Staff or the Department's overall Law and Organization Bureau within the Secretariat General. The draft SK is then sent up to the Director General or Minister, depending on who is issuing it. When the SK in question involves the interests of more than one Directorate or Directorate General, an internal team is formed to provide a vehicle for coordination. Where other government Departments or Agencies may be affected or involved, an inter-departmental team is set up. In some cases, inter-departmental efforts result in a Joint SK involving two or more Ministers. Usually, at official meetings of these coordination teams, agreements hammered out earlier in informal discussions are formalized. Some Provincial regulations also bear on forestry policy, but these are generally of a derivative and technical nature.

Coordination in rule-making is intermittent at best, and SKs, government regulations, and even basic laws often overlap and contradict

---

political integration and control at the local level. The primary political thrust of New Order development policies in rural areas over the past 25 years has thus been to depoliticize the villages in the hope of making them more amenable to state political control and to the delivery of such services as education and healthcare. (Barber, 1989)

At the same time, officials are well aware that rural development activities typically fail if local people don't lend at least passive support, in exchange for which they must receive some benefits from development. Donor agencies have also urged "increased community participation" on the government in many contexts, both because they believe that community support is essential

to success and because it is in line with the Western political traditions that influence the officials themselves and the non-governmental groups in their home countries that scrutinize their activities abroad.

As a result of this uneasy balance in the forestry sector, many official policy documents extol the virtues of "participation," even while existing laws and policies severely limit the meaning of the term as applied. The Indonesian Forestry Action Programme, for example, argues that "there is a need for transforming the traditional biological-cum-financial approach in forestry to a more broadly-based socio-economic approach in order to support locally sustainable each other. Compilations of forestry regulations are published sporadically (GOI, 1970–1990), but there is no systematic process for cataloguing regulations or determining to what extent a new regulation voids an old one, and laws are not indexed or cross-referenced. As a result, Indonesia has amassed more than 1,800 pages of law and regulation on forestry that is often difficult to draw authoritative meaning or guidance from.

Ironically, significant gaps in forestry laws and regulations still remain. The relationship of customary *adat* law to national forestry regulation, for example, has never been legislatively clarified, and so conflict in the field, where these laws are applied, continues. Indonesia also lacks an independent process for interpreting vague or debatable law or regulation authoritatively. By definition, the Elucidations and explanatory memorandums that always accompany Basic Laws and government regulations can't resolve unforeseen situations.

The judiciary plays virtually no role in interpreting laws and regulations. It can neither offer authoritative interpretations of disputed provisions nor strike down legislation or regulations as unconstitutional. (Vatakiotis, 1989; Lev, 1977) In any case, the judiciary is part of the executive branch, so it lacks the independence to conduct review of legislation. Since no other institution possesses this authority either, the bureaucracy itself becomes the *de facto* "court of last resort." As one government official who helps draft legislation notes, "people don't start with basic concepts of law—the law is only one form of political position-taking." (Vatakiotis, 1989)

This state of affairs benefits two stakeholders in forest policy-making. Forestry officials themselves benefit, since the indeterminacy of law and regulation—and the lack of an external review mechanism—mean that those who interpret and administer the rules have greater power. Second, those with access to and influence on the apparatus benefit, primarily large private firms.

economic development, with due consideration given to maximizing meaningful participation of the people." (GOI, 1991) On the other hand, not one Indonesian forest policy document addresses the need to reform the many laws on land rights, forms of village organization, and forestry.

Non-governmental organizations (NGOs) have also found their access to forest policy-making limited. Under pressure from some aid donors, NGO participation has increased in those policy forums where such donors hold sway *(See Box 4.3)*, but NGOs have no systematic way to provide input to forest policy-making and to comment on pending decisions or regulations, and the Ministry of Forestry is not required to respond publicly to questions raised by NGOs, citizens, or anyone else outside the formal apparatus.

To increase their access and participation, NGOs have taken their case to the national media, the Parliament, and, working through Northern-based environmental NGOs, to donors and the international media. Success has been limited, however. Although the national media has grown bolder since the late 1980s, traditionally sensitive issues, such as land rights in forest areas, economic concentration in the forestry industry, and the like, are still subject to *de facto* censorship. Occasionally, the parliament raises sticky issues, getting them more media attention than NGOs could on

Box 4.3. Participation by Non-Governmental Organizations (NGOs) in The Tropical Forestry Action Program in Indonesia

The Tropical Forestry Action Program (TFAP) has failed to involve non-governmental organizations (NGOs) in many of the countries where the plan has been carried out since the mid-1980s. (Cort, 1991) The "top-down" nature of the international program itself is partly to blame (Colchester and Lohmann, 1990; Winterbottom, 1990), but the weaknesses of national-level participatory norms and mechanisms are also at fault. Indonesia is a case in point.

In 1988, the World Bank funded an "Indonesia Forestry Institutions and Conservation Project" managed by the Ministry of Forestry with help from FAO consultants. As part of the project, forty Forestry Studies were completed and, in late 1990, synthesized into four volumes (GOI/FAO, 1990) that provided the basic information, proposals, and documents needed to develop the national TFAP. Two national Roundtables were held in May 1990 and February 1992 on successive versions of the national plan.

Whether NGOs would participate in the 1990 Roundtable remained uncertain until several weeks before the meeting. Both the Ministry of Forestry and FAO initially resisted the idea. The Secretariat of the Indonesian Forum on the Environment (WALHI)—an umbrella group for some 400 or more NGOs—received its invitation and accompanying documentation only five days before the Roundtable, and the Indonesian Forest Conservation Network (SKEPHI) was invited only 24 hours in advance. The NGOs were given little time to prepare, each was allowed only ten minutes to speak, and their written presentations were not included in the minutes of the meeting. Backed by several donors, WALHI called for the establishment of a broad-based working group to revise the draft document, but no such group was created. Concerns raised about equity, popular participation, land tenure and other policy reforms, needs for a more cross-sectoral orientation, and needs for more emphasis on biodiversity conservation were not formally responded to at the Roundtable, or afterwards.

The forty Forestry Studies documents were displayed—wrapped in plastic—but were not made available, and though they were later leaked, their distribution still remains restricted, as does that of the Synthesis Report; these documents produced in English only, further restricting access. Summary documents produced in English and Indonesian in late 1990 (GOI, 1990) were so brief that the basis of the policy plans and the process by which they were developed can't be analyzed critically.

The 1992 Roundtable held to discuss the final version of the Action Plan (GOI, 1991) was somewhat more participatory: NGOs were invited to take part and received documentation in advance, some of which they translated themselves. Yet, the government did not address the policy issues the NGOs raised—including the issues of tenure, the distribution of the costs and benefits of forest management, and public participation—and major donors would discuss policy questions and project funding only with Ministry officials and only in private. In short, though public participation in the TFAP process has widened, most serious discussion and policy-making still takes place behind closed doors.

their own, but in Indonesia's strong Presidential system, the Indonesian parliament has relatively little power. And while recruiting the assistance of Northern environmental NGOs to lobby on specific projects has worked in some cases, bringing in outsiders can also prompt government officials to dig in their heels on an issue on grounds of patriotism. Indeed, provisions of a 1992 Law on Immigration allow government to prevent citizens who had criticized the government while overseas from returning home and to revoke their citizenship. (Aznam, 1992b)

Over-arching all NGO activities in Indonesia is the 1985 Law on Societal Organizations, which holds that NGO activity is legitimate only to the extent that it conforms to the official *Pancasila* ideology, and to the goals and programs of national development.[2] In short, an NGO's existence and activities depends on state approval, which is granted only to non-political organizations that take *Pancasila* as their sole principle and devote themselves to national development as defined by the authorities.

However constrained, NGOs clearly have options. In contrast, local communities influence policy mainly through what Scott called "the weapons of the weak"—everyday forms of peasant resistance, such as ignoring forest boundaries to farm or collect forest products, ripping out tree seedlings planted by state foresters, setting fires, and the like. (Peluso, 1988; Scott, 1985)

Neither of these strategies has had much impact on policy. The work of NGOs has raised the profile of many problems in the current policy framework, but so far few policy-makers take these new upstart organizations seriously, and their lack of access to information, their limited capacities and skills, and the restrictions imposed by laws on non-governmental social and political speech and action all pose constraints. Peasant resistance, on the other hand, has been extremely effective in rendering many state forest policies ineffective, from reforestation schemes to protection of nature reserves. But resistance, by its very nature, provides no coherent policy alternatives.

Restrictions on information within the forestry sector both attest to and reaffirm the exclusive nature of the policy process in Indonesia. Only the officials of the Ministry of Forestry are allowed to see documents related to pending projects or actions, even those sponsored by outside donors.

For instance, World Bank documents, which often contain the most up-to-date and comprehensive general data available on the forestry sector, as well as key information on pending project decisions, are officially confidential. They are particularly closely guarded when key decisions are being made—just when NGOs and the public at large most need the information.

Official forest policy-makers themselves often lack vital information. True to bureaucratic form, what is reported upward through the ranks often disguises problems in the field and generally accords with what policy-makers want to hear. Since a dispute between a timber concession-holder and a local community, for example, might reflect poorly on a local official unable to resolve it swiftly, the official naturally downplays the problem. (Barber 1989) The net effect of thousands of such acts of bureaucratic "spin control" is to distort policy-makers' views of the specific impacts of their policies.

Structural Ignorance

Reform of Indonesian forest policy-making is also stymied by "structural ignorance"—defined by Dove (1988) as "the failure to perceive that which is not in one's own best interests to perceive." Too often in policy-making, some players perpetuate unfounded—or at least widely contested—assumptions and assertions that support the *status quo*. Although such myths are generally not the actual cause of environment and development problems, they impede solutions because they blind decision-makers to empirical evidence—no matter how solid—that contradicts them.

One unproven assumption enshrined in both the Constitution and the Basic Forestry Law of 1967 is that prevailing forest policies benefit "the national interest." Accordingly, forestry officials consider rural communities or others who oppose current policies to be ignorant, misled, misinformed, or, in some cases, politically motivated and subversive. Conflicts over forest policy are thus framed as "conflicts between the welfare of the country as a whole and the self-indulgence of one particular group" and as "conflicts between national development and backwards peasant culture" (Dove, 1988: 32), even though peasant resistance to policies such as the timber concession system is, in fact, "a simple matter of the peasants defending their personal interests against the equally personal interests of the policy-makers." (Dove, 1988: 31, 32)

The way that the costs and benefits of particular forestry sector policies and projects are evaluated in policy discourse also misrepresents reality. Nearly all Indonesian forestry policy-makers fail to perceive the true opportunity costs to rural people of limiting their access to forest lands and resources and of taking their land out of production. Even when monetary compensation is paid by government agencies or timber concession-holders, it is usually a fraction of the actual value of the resource—in effect, a token payment, as in the case of Dusunpulau village in Sumatra's Bengkulu province. *(See Box 4.4.)*

At the same time, inflated views of the benefits of forest development policies and projects prompt forestry officials to dismiss or patronize peasants who don't concur:

According to this view, peasant resistance to development projects is due not to the possibility that a project was planned without regard for the peasants' own interests, but rather to the fact that the project was simply not completely understood by (or adequately explained to) them...[T]he possibility of government error is thereby categorized out of existence: there are no bad projects and mistreated peasants, but only "misunderstood" projects and "misunderstanding" peasants. (Dove, 1988: 29)

Strengthening this view is the attitude of many forest policy-makers that traditional societies in Indonesia cling to wasteful resource-management practices that will never deliver them from poverty. Official policies that discourage traditional swidden agriculture systems of the Outer Islands are indicative of this view.

Despite mounting scientific evidence that some forms of swidden are environmentally appropriate and sensible in many Indonesian settings (Weinstock 1990), if combined with well-managed agro-forestry and adequate access to land—and despite evidence that few alternative cropping systems are ecologically feasible for many marginal lands (NRC 1993)—the Indonesian government's line on these practices continues to echo colonial assessments: that swidden and its practitioners are environmentally unsustainable, destructive, and wasteful. In the country's basic land and forest laws, this view is institutionalized: all forms of land under swidden cultivation are considered "abandoned" and thus ineligible for ownership. (Zerner, 1990; Barber and Churchill, 1987)

This purblind view of swidden-based forest societies persists because the belief that the forest is an empty and dangerous territory, unproductive in its natural state, runs deep in the culture and history of the Javanese—Indonesia's demographically, culturally, and politically dominant ethnic group. A continuing concern of the early Javanese kingdoms was to open up forests for new agricultural lands: "Just as cleared land became associated with the rise of the Javanese states and their cultures, so too did the forest come to be associated with uncivilized, uncontrollable, and fearful forces." (Dove, 1985) But if the swidden cultivators of those times were not under the control of the courts, and swidden cultivators on forest lands were poorly integrated into the body politic and the economy during the colonial period when swidden was characterized as a "robber economy" (Colchester, 1990) the current blanket condemnation of swidden (GOI, 1991) reflects mainly cultural myth—the Javanese preference for the settled wet-rice cultivation systems of Java. (Dove, 1985) This myth also justifies the transfer of rights in the forest from traditional shifting cultivators to timber concession-holders and others with vested interests in the government's model of forest development.

Swidden cultivation's bad reputation isn't deserved. Generally, this form of agriculture is only one part of a household livelihood strategy that

Box 4.4. The Uncounted Costs of Logging in Dusunpulau Village, Sumatra

Governments and timber companies alike underestimate the costs that logging operations visit on many forest-dependent villages. The experience of Dusunpulau Village in Sumatra's Bengkulu Province provides a stark but typical example. What is rare is that the villagers brought their case to court in September 1993, claiming losses amounting to some $3.8 million, and demanding compensation.

For at least 100 years, Dusunpulau's residents have tapped damar trees (*Shorea javanica*) to get readily-marketable resin. Indeed, their written *adat* claims over damar trees around their settlement date back to 1883. For generations, the trees have provided these villagers with supplementary cash income. "Since I was little, I have appreciated the damar trees," said Dahlan, a local farmer who owned 200 damar trees before they were cut down by the logging company. "School fees, for example, were never a problem for my parents, as long as they could tap the resin."

The income from damar is indeed significant. Every three months, a mature damar tree can yield 15 kilograms of resin, which can be easily sold for 60 cents per kilo. Over a year, one such tree thus potentially yields some $36. Dahlan's annual cash income from his 200 trees thus might reach $7,000, more than ten times the average per capita national income. Once past prime age for resin tapping, the harvested timber also fetches about $75 per cubic meter.

In 1974, the PT Maju Jaya Raya Timber company obtained a 20-year HPH concession covering some 80,000 hectares directly adjacent to Dusunpulau village. For some years, the company did not interfere with the villagers' continued resin tapping in their *adat* forests, though those forests lie within the official boundaries of the timber concession. In recent years, however, the company cut down the community's damar trees—3,950 by the community's count—and took the timber away. "We couldn't stop them," said Dahlan, "because they were supported by the government security apparatus."

The community complained to local government officials, and the *Bupati* (Regent) asked the company to settle the matter. (A 1974 Ministerial Decree holds that *adat* rights to harvest forest products—such as damar resin—should be respected, but in this case the company's right to harvest timber conflicts directly with the community's *adat* right to harvest the resin from the very same trees.) The timber company, however, was only willing to provide $1,000 in cash and about $1,750 to build a village mosque, an offer that "has no connection with the demands for compensation," according to the villagers' attorney.

The company's management, however, considers the villagers' compensation claim as baseless, and the company's attorney claims that "there is no damar growing in the concession area…only untended trees" and that "before the concession was established, that area was thick forest that people could not possibly enter." Not so, says Zulkifli, another aggrieved villager: "This forest is the source of our livelihood, so going into the forest has always been our daily work. Indeed, it is only these people in neckties and cars that are unable to enter the forest."

While awaiting the outcome of the court case (which could take a year or more), Dusunpulau villagers are farming subsistence crops along the edges of their former damar forest, which no longer exists.

Source: Syukur, 1993.

might also include gathering of forest products, wage employment, cultivation of long-rotation tree crops, such as damar (*Shorea javanica*), and sedentary farming. As traditionally practiced, such "diversified portfolio" systems—used by as many as six million people, mainly in Kalimantan and Sumatra—have been "relatively stable and self-sustaining" in Indonesia. (FAO/GOI, 1990 Vol. 4, 24)

Officially, the government distinguishes traditional swidden practitioners from "forest squatters"—typically, poor and landless people from lowland rural or urban areas who follow logging roads or other entry points into the forest in search of a living. Most so-called squatters have little knowledge of the local forest environment, grow mainly such cash crops as pepper or cinnamon, and use land continuously until its fertility is exhausted, with no intention of returning to a particular plot once it is used. Unfortunately, "it is not possible to distinguish the two groups in a meaningful way in the field" (FAO/GOI, 1990, Vol. 4, 29), and the official solution has therefore been to convert all "shifting cultivators" to sedentary farmers, either *in situ*, or after resettlement.

Government views are changing, however. A noted Indonesian social scientist and senior official in the National Development Planning Agency recently noted that traditional shifting cultivation is an environmentally sound and productive land use that should be distinguished from the activities of "forest scavengers." Traditional systems, he noted, were under pressure from these scavengers and competition for land from commercial interests—pressures compounded by government attempts to control traditional ways of life in inappropriate ways. These policies frustrate forest farmers, he concluded, and create the false impression that they are enemies of the forest. (*Indonesian Observer*, 1993)

Despite some changing attitudes, a range of government programs is aimed at dismantling traditional swidden-based societies. Indeed, in 1993 the former Ministry of Transmigration was renamed the "Ministry of Transmigration and Resettlement of Forest Squatters," which promptly

announced a plan to resettle 10,000 "forest squatter" families. (*Jakarta Post*, 1993b)

The experience of traditional villagers with the *HPH Bina Desa* program (hereafter *Bina Desa*) in the Bukit Baka/Bukit Raya National Park area of west and central Kalimantan illustrates the day-to-day impacts of structural ignorance on forest communities. Promulgated by the Ministry of Forestry in 1991, *Bina Desa* requires concession-holders to undertake rural development activities to acquire and maintain their licenses. A main objective of *Bina Desa* is to convince local communities to abandon swidden in favor of sedentary wet-rice farming. The concession-holder supplies seed, pesticide, and sporadic extension services, and Javanese transmigrants are brought in from other areas to demonstrate "proper" agriculture. A recent field assessment in the area concluded the following about the program:

> Wet rice cultivation may indeed have the potential for economic and ecological sustainability in certain niches. However, farmers now participating in [the program] are dependent on agricultural inputs supplied by the concessionaire, and intensive fertilizer use has led to a proliferation of weeds in the dryland rice fields. Pesticide use without proper instruction has adverse implications for ecological and human health. The negative psychological impact of concessionaire (and government) attempts to change traditional practices is palpable in the project area. Farmers now refer to their own agricultural system as *perladangan liar*, a pejorative term meaning "wild cultivation." (Seymour et al., 1993)

Inevitably, traditional shifting cultivation practices will change in coming decades as increasing demands for food production and decreasing per capita land availability fuel the drive to intensify food production. Moreover, traditional agriculture systems have never been static—witness the relatively recent addition of rubber to Indonesian swiddeners' crop portfolios. There is much to build on in the diverse traditional systems employed throughout

Indonesia. But until the blanket condemnation of swidden as "backward and unproductive" is laid to rest, it will be very difficult to develop new hybrid systems that combine the best of traditional and modern systems and allow increased food production in and on the fringes of fragile rainforest ecosystems.

A final set of myths also influences forest policy. Too often, policy-makers equate natural, intact tropical rainforests with industrial timber plantations, even though these two ecosystems differ radically in terms of biological diversity, goods, and services. While tree farms are needed to supply fiber for industry, they are not nearly as biologically rich or as economically valuable to local communities as natural forests.

The distorted discourse on the costs and benefits of alternative forest-management policies and strategies combines with a legal morass and a lack of popular participation to insulate the forest policy-making process in Indonesia from criticism, narrow the range of alternatives that are seriously discussed, and perpetuate existing policies. Add the lobbying of the forest industry and the Indonesian forestry bureaucracy's efforts to maintain the existing system, and it is not surprising that change is slow in coming.

Forest Policy-making in the United States

In the United States, the complex forest policy-making process reflects a century of legislative attempts to balance tensions between the exploitation of forest resources and their conservation. Compared to Indonesia, policy-making is relatively decentralized and broad-based. Legislation affecting forests is considered by a variety of Congressional committees and by state legislatures, while policy and regulatory decisions are made by state and federal agencies at various levels. But though forest planning processes and policy changes are often structured to allow public comment, and the United States has "checks and balances" not found in Indonesia, forest policy-making has not yet struck a balance needed to sustain the many valued assets and services provided by the Pacific Northwest's forest ecosystems.

In the Northwest, the National Forests are the major policy battleground. They contain most of the remaining natural forest ecosystems, provide the region with its most important wildlife habitats and reservoirs of biodiversity, protect vital watersheds that provide municipal and agricultural water, and permit public recreation and scientific research[3]—goods and services that intensively managed private timber lands can no longer provide. At the same time, the public has a far greater say over what happens on public lands than it does on private lands.[4] Then too, the history of forestry innovation and reform in the United States suggests that the Forest Service introduces most major changes in forestry.

For the first four decades after their creation, the National Forests were managed as forest reserves. The Organic Act of 1897 and the Transfer Act of 1905 (which transferred federal forest reserves from the Department of Interior to the Department of Agriculture) gave the U.S. Forest Service its principal and rather simple management mission—to improve and protect the forests, to manage the forests for water supplies, and to furnish a continuous supply of timber, in that order. The agency mainly protected the forests from fires, pests, and timber poachers and carried out other custodial duties. Since most timber needs could be met on private lands, demand for timber from the National Forests was minimal. (Clary, 1986) Most new federal laws affecting the U.S. Forest Service during the agency's first few decades simply expanded its geographic area or directed it to increase forestry research and implement cooperative forest programs with state and private landowners.

Government's custodial role ended as demands for wood products rose during the Second World War and the ensuing post-war housing boom. As supplies of old-growth and mature timber on private lands dwindled, production was stepped up in the National Forests nationwide, from less than 1.5 billion boardfeet in 1941, timber production grew to 12.8 billion boardfeet by

1968. (Sample and LeMaster, 1992; O'Toole, 1988) In the Northwest, annual harvest levels reached 4.5 billion boardfeet in the National Forests by the 1960s. Totals ranged from 3.1 (during the 1981–83 recession) to 5.5 billion board feet (in the late 1980s) annually for over 25 years before a 1991 federal court injunction halted most federal timber sales in the Northwest until the northern spotted owl habitat is adequately protected.

By the 1950s, however, it became clear that logging on National Forests could threaten other public non-timber forest resources, such as water, fisheries, wildlife, soil, and recreation. (Lyden et al., 1990) In 1960, on the recommendation of the U.S. Forest Service, Congress passed the Multiple-Use Sustained-Yield Act, which expanded the agency's management mandate to include forest resources beyond water and timber. For the first time, the Forest Service was directed to manage the National Forest system for outdoor recreation, range, fish and wildlife, and wilderness, in addition to watershed and timber uses. Moreover, the Act defined "sustained-yield" to cover not just timber but other renewable forest resources as well. *(See Box 4.5.)* Yet, though the Multiple-Use

Sustained-Yield Act (MUSY) was a major landmark in forest legislation, its implementation was left largely to the discretion of the Forest Service. Indeed, in a 1979 ruling, the U.S. Ninth Circuit Court of Appeals concluded that the Act "breathes discretion at every pore."[5] Controversies over extensive clearcutting in Montana, West Virginia, and elsewhere during the early 1970s convinced many conservationists that the MUSY alone could not protect non-timber resources. Congress eventually agreed, and first passed the Forest and Rangelands Resource Planning Act in 1974 and then the National Forest Management Act in 1976 to address MUSY's weaknesses.

The Forest and Rangelands Resource Planning Act (RPA) requires the Forest Service to develop a long-range national strategic plan to assure the long-term sustainable management of all renewable forest resources in the National Forest system. This plan, updated every five years,[6] requires the agency to set clear goals and objectives for a range of forest resources from timber to wildlife, wilderness, and recreation, and to budget what's needed to implement them. For the

---

Box 4.5. The Multiple Use-Sustained Yield Act of 1960

The most important parts of the Multiple Use-Sustained Yield Act are its definitions of "multiple use" and "sustained yield." Their interpretation fuels much of the debate over Forest Service mandates and reforms. Section 4 of the Act defines the terms as follows:

(a) "Multiple use" means the management of all the various renewable surface resources of the National Forests so that they are utilized in the combination that will best meet the needs of the American people; making the judicious use of land for some or all of these resources or related services over areas large enough to provide sufficient latitude for periodic adjustments in use to conform to changing needs and condi-

tions; that some land will be used for less than all of the resources; and harmonious and coordinated management of the various resources, each with the other, without impairment of the productivity of the land, with consideration being given to the relative values of the various resources, and not necessarily the combination of uses that will give the greatest dollar return or the greatest unit output.

(b) "Sustained yield of the several products and services" means the achievement and maintenance in perpetuity of a high-level annual or regular periodic output of the various renewable resources of the National Forests without impairment of the productivity of the land.

basic assessment and each update, renewable resources on Forest Service lands are inventoried, then analyzed in terms of supply-and-demand for the next 50 years. Finally, policies and regulations that might affect all forest land owners are proposed, enabling Congress to keep long-term goals and the big picture in mind as it makes shorter-term policy and budget decisions.

The National Forest Management Act (NFMA) essentially amended the RPA, extending long-range planning to the local level.[7] For each National Forest, the law requires a detailed, ten-year land-and-resource-management plan. The Act tries to promote sustainable forest management by restricting timber operations on lands physically and economically unfit for such use.[8] Under NFMA-mandated planning, several management alternatives are produced, typically ranging from preserving non-timber forest services to the intensive production of timber or other commodities. The idea is to integrate "top-down" RPA planning with "bottom-up" perspectives. Congress, hoping to avoid making controversial decisions itself, built public participation into the legislation in the belief that conflicts would be resolved during the planning process.

Despite the intent of the MUSY, RPA, and NFMA, the Forest Service and Congress continued to emphasize logging at the expense of other forest resources. In the Northwest, harvest levels were raised to record volumes during the mid-1980s (Haynes, 1992) despite clear evidence (e.g., Thomas et al., 1993; Gordon et al., 1991; Norse, 1990; Anderson and Gerhke, 1988) that heavy harvests were already seriously damaging water quality and fish and wildlife habitat and threatening endangered species.

As the status of old-growth forest ecosystems and the wildlife that inhabit them became better understood during the 1980s, environmental groups charged that the U.S. Forest Service was violating NFMA, the National Environmental Policy Act (NEPA), and other environmental laws. When the agency planned to continue harvesting old-growth forests at annual rates of nearly 25,000 hectares without an approved

protection plan for the northern spotted owl, as required by the NFMA, the conflict entered the courts. (Bonnet and Zimmerman, 1991)

In a series of rulings, the federal courts have found the U.S. Fish and Wildlife Service,[9] the U.S. Forest Service,[10] and the Bureau of Land Management[11] in violation of various environmental laws intended to protect endangered species and other forest resources in the Pacific Northwest.[12] On May 23, 1991, U.S. Judge William Dwyer barred logging in northern spotted owl habitat until the federal government came up with a scientifically and legally sound species-protection plan. (*Seattle Audubon Society v. Evans*) The judge's statement was unusually blunt:

> The records in this case…show a remarkable series of violations of the environmental laws…More is involved here than a simple failure of an agency to comply with its governing statute. The most recent violation of the NFMA exemplified a deliberate and systematic refusal by the Forest Service and the FWS [U.S. Fish and Wildlife Service] to comply with laws protecting wildlife.

When the Forest Service submitted a protection plan in March 1992, the court rejected it because it failed to consider new information on declining owl populations and other species dependent on old-growth ecosystems. The permanent injunction on logging remained in place.

Why did high timber harvest levels continue despite growing public opposition, legal reforms, and scientific evidence that intensive logging is seriously damaging the Northwest's forest ecosystems and their diverse resources? Two other questions come first: who are the dominant beneficiaries of current forest policies on the National Forests? And what aspects of policy-making work against forest policy reform?

Who Benefits from High Harvest Levels?

In the Northwest, three interest groups benefit most from the heavy timber harvests that threaten National Forests' ability to sustain a variety of forest resources. First, the forest industry enjoys subsidized access to public timber supplies—including the large sawlogs available on few private lands. Second, timber-processing facilities, employment, and local government revenues from the sale of federal timber benefit some local communities. Third, the Forest Service benefits from high harvest levels because budgets and performance incentives are tied to timber sales.

Most forest industry firms, whether or not they own land, benefit from heavy harvests on federal lands. Although reduced timber supplies on federal lands have increased the value of timber on private lands, there are several reasons why the timber industry has been relatively unified in its bid to keep public timber harvest levels high. Subsidized road construction is part of a winning bidder's bounty. In 1991, the U.S. Forest Service spent nearly $190 million in road construction (OMB, 1992), much of it in the Pacific Northwest. In 1987, 100-percent reimbursable road credits totaled $21 million dollars in just two Oregon National Forests (Willamette and Umpqua). (Gorte, 1989)

In parts of the country where timber sale receipts are less than road-construction and other timber-sale costs, the road-construction subsidy is more obvious than it is in the Northwest, where timber sales generally surpass timber sale administration costs (including roads).[13] Either way, road credits amount to short-term, interest-free loans since they can be used instead of cash to pay for the federal timber (OTA, 1992), and purchasers can transfer credits among timber sales in the same National Forest (but not between Forests or between purchasers), effectively extending the loan's term.

Many firms have benefited from the availability of large supplies of public timber in other ways, too. Until the mid-1980s, a purchaser of National Forest timber had five years to harvest the sale with no down payment. This allowed timber companies to purchase large quantities when prices were relatively low and to harvest when prices increased. Moreover, when timber prices plummeted during the recession of the early 1980s, Senator Mark Hatfield of Oregon pushed Congress to extend the performance of the contracts by two years to help companies that had purchased large amounts of federal timber in the late 1970s avoid bankruptcy. In contrast, on private lands, timber sale contracts usually call for a substantial down-payment and give concessionaires only one year to harvest. In other words, federal timber supplies and sales procedures have allowed timber companies to speculate on timber prices while taking virtually no risks. Although abuses of this system did spark some reforms in the mid-1980s—now sold timber must be harvested within three years and a 5 percent down payment is required—opportunities for almost risk-free speculation remain.

Smaller firms—especially companies with no land of their own—benefit from federal timber too because they have little access to alternative supplies. Because they lack the investment capital and assets to finance the technological changes needed to use second-growth trees efficiently, their profit margin often rises and falls with their access to large sawtimber—most of which is on National Forest lands. (Olson, 1988)

The longstanding ban on the export of federal logs benefits both large and small timber companies. Since timber from the National Forests cannot be exported, a dual timber market has developed in the Northwest—a domestic market and a higher-priced export market. Flora and colleagues (1989) estimate that export logs in 1988 sold for between $25 and $400 more per thousand boardfeet (for second-growth small-diameter spruce and for high-grade old-growth, respectively) than logs sold on the domestic market.[14] The partial export ban effectively enlarges the domestic timber supply (lowering prices) and serves as a form of international trade protection for inefficient producers—many of them either smaller independent companies or older mills owned by larger companies. As federal timber supplies have been reduced following the federal court logging injunctions, the inefficient producers have been affected most severely.

Because the ban does not apply to timber from private lands,[15] land-owning companies (and smaller non-industrial owners) enjoy higher international market prices for the timber they do legally export. Since the United States is the dominant supplier of softwood logs to the world market,[16] private American log producers—most of them in the Pacific Northwest—almost control international softwood log prices (Sedjo et al., 1992), and in 1991, log exports from Washington state alone were worth over $1.35 billion.[17] (Washington Office of Financial Management, 1991)

Despite federal laws designed to prevent direct substitution by allowing log-exporting mills to purchase federal logs only from third parties, indirect substitution is apparently common. Without large supplies of public timber, forest industry representatives have claimed they would have to close mills and lay off thousands of workers. (Rasmussen, et al., 1991; Beuter, 1990) Yet, during the 1980s and early 1990s, timber exports from Oregon and Washington exceeded 3 billion boardfeet,[18] most of it from forest industry lands. (Adams and Haynes, 1990) This volume is equivalent to 50 percent of the total sawtimber harvest on forest industry lands west of the Cascades and just under the 1980–89 average harvest on the National Forests. To the extent that substitution occurs, these firms can sell their own supplies for higher prices and then use lower-cost public timber to feed regional processing operations. And federal tax credits give log exporters an estimated $100 million in annual tax breaks on top of the record international prices they have enjoyed in recent years. (Oregonian, 1993a)

Local governments also benefit enormously from high harvest levels on the National Forests. Since 1908, the Forest Service has shared revenues from timber sales, recreation, minerals, and other sources with local governments (mainly counties), based on net receipts. In 1976, the same year in which NFMA passed, Congress approved a little-noticed amendment to the 1964 National Forest Roads and Trails Act that raised the revenue sharing with counties to 25 percent of gross receipts to compensate for tax revenues that would be paid if the land were privately owned. But many counties in western Oregon and Washington have

received far more from the Forest Service than they would have collected in taxes on the same amount of land. (O'Toole, 1988)

Since over 80 percent of Forest Service revenues come from timber sales,[19] many counties want high harvest levels maintained. In 1988, counties in Washington and Oregon collected over $220 million from National Forest timber sales. Afraid of losing these revenues just when other federal assistance has waned, local governments in the Northwest have opposed efforts to reduce harvest levels in the National Forests. Indeed, many have lobbied to maintain or increase federal timber sales, even at the expense of other resources and industries. (Sample, 1990)

And, not least, the Forest Service has benefited from high timber-harvest levels on the forest lands it manages because budget levels are tied to timber production. Since Congress traditionally allocates more than 80 percent of the Forest Service project budget to road construction, timber management, and timber sale activities (OTA, 1990), forest supervisors have an obvious incentive to orient planning toward timber production.[20] Jobs also depend on the status quo. By February 1993, the agency was considering abolishing hundreds of timber-related jobs in the agency, citing the court-ordered injunction against harvesting in spotted owl habitat. (Greenwire, 1993)

The Knutson-Vandenberg Act in 1930 gives the Forest Service still another incentive to keep timber harvest levels high. This act allows the agency to retain some of the proceeds from timber sales (K-V Funds) to carry out reforestation and silvicultural management on the forest where the harvest took place. In 1976, the NFMA amended the act to allow the use of K-V funds for wildlife management, environmental education, and other chronically under-funded activities. In other words, forest managers have to cut trees to save wildlife habitat.

As O'Toole (1988) points out, "Forest Service managers who wish to increase their budgets will discover that they can use their [Congressional] appropriations to sell timber and collect more K-V funds." OTA (1992) found no evidence that these permanent appropriations are efficient or necessary for improving forest management, but did conclude that they influence managers to increase timber harvests to increase budgets. Moreover, Congress exercises virtually no oversight or control of K-V funds and other permanent, discretionary accounts. (OTA, 1992)

Finally, the relatively "profitable" and high-volume timber sales in U.S. Forest Service Region 6 (Oregon and Washington) have also given the agency political benefits. Since timber sales in other regions of the country lose money for the federal treasury (O'Toole, 1988; Repetto, 1988), the timber sold in Region 6 contributes the bulk of the approximately $400 million returned to the Treasury each year from National Forest revenues. If these sales were curtailed,[21] the agency would lose much more than the $300 to $400 million it has been losing annually on timber sales nationwide—perhaps another $250 million or more. Political pressure to make the agency manage its assets more productively is growing, and timber sales in the Northwest make the bottom line look a little less dismal.

A Forest Policy Process Divided Against Itself

Several features of the American political process have enabled the principal beneficiaries of high harvest levels to maintain or expand their benefits during the past decade. First, short-term policies that determine harvest are out of sync with long-term policies intended to protect forest resources. Second, key aspects of forest policy-making have been dominated by timber interests despite the increasing influence of environmental groups. Third, the forest-planning process is so complex that public involvement is limited. Finally, as in Indonesia, the *status quo* is supported by the embrace of unproven assumptions and the selective use of facts in policy debates and political discourse. All too often, the emphasis is on how to protect forestry and forest industries from change, not on how to sustain natural forest ecosystems.

Federal forest policy is made in three ways. First, long-term management goals and planning processes are legislated in acts such as MUSY, NEPA, RPA, and NFMA. These laws are intended to provide an overall policy framework to ensure the long-range sustainability of all renewable resources in National Forests. Second, on an annual basis, short-term policies are established as the budget requests of the U.S. Forest Service and the administration are prepared, negotiated, and Congressionally approved. Third, the federal courts make forest policy when laws are not carried out, or when Congress and the Executive have not taken actions to resolve conflicts or ambiguities in the Federal laws that govern the use and management of National Forests.

In theory, the policies manifested in the annual budget and appropriations are to reflect the sustainability issues identified and addressed in the RPA program and in the National Forest management plans mandated by NFMA. In practice, annual appropriations don't reflect long-term policies to promote the sustainable management of all forest resources. The Forest Service doesn't provide Congress with specific and credible information on critical sustainability issues, or suggest budgetary priorities for addressing them. Congress isn't blameless either: it focuses narrowly in annual appropriations legislation on timber sale targets and largely ignores many of the other programs in the budget that are crucial to meeting the requirements of NEPA, RPA, and the NFMA. The U.S. Office of Technology Assessment (OTA) concludes that the RPA, the act most directly concerned with the forests' use and future, has so far been a failure despite significant improvements in some areas covered by the law. In its summary, OTA (1990) states:

> RPA Assessments have suffered from poor data on resource conditions and the analyses of opportunities and threats have been incomplete. RPA Programs have provided neither sufficient guidance for annual budgets nor clear direction for agency activities. Annual Reports have provided inadequate feedback on implementation. And neither the administration nor Congress has

demonstrated sufficient commitment to make the process work.

The OTA report notes that while timber resource assessments are relatively complete (with the exception of those on old-growth forests), most RPA assessments of recreation, rangeland, water, wildlife, and wilderness resources are not. Most troubling is the lack of information on resource quality and trends in the RPA inventories, since program analyses are based on this information. Also, Congress's review of Forest Service management and administrative programs is inadequately linked to the resource assessments. Congress appropriates less than two thirds of the Forest Service budget each year. The remainder of the Agency's budget comes from special trust funds or permanent appropriations accounts created by Congress to allow the Forest Service to use some of its revenues from the sale of timber and other resources. Since nearly all of these permanent appropriations are tied to the timber sale program (OTA, 1990), the other two thirds of the Agency's budget comes from funds that are competing with other federal programs. If Congress has no budget priorities to follow and simply cuts annual Forest Service appropriations across the board, the non-timber programs lose out because they are not protected by trust funds and special accounts (financed by timber revenues not returned to the Federal treasury).

Although Congress passed laws such as the MUSY, RPA, and NFMA to protect non-timber values, it has also perpetuated intensive timber exploitation at the expense of other forest resources. There are two main explanations for this seeming inconsistency. First, through the yearly budget appropriations process, Congress sets annual timber-harvest targets for the National Forests.[22] Politically determined, these harvest levels often exceed realistic expectations based on the available timber base, past harvest levels, and environmental considerations mandated by federal law. Second, by focussing the appropriations process and mandates for the use of National Forest revenues on the timber program, Congress has created stronger incentives for the Forest Service to "get the cut out" than to

meet the environmental requirements of various laws.

Ideally, the budget proposals presented by the U.S. Forest Service and prepared under the guidance of the RPA and the NFMA would reflect a "balance" between commodity-management programs and programs aimed at preserving water, fisheries, wildlife and recreation. Indeed, the NFMA requires the agency to design its resource management programs in an integrated fashion. (For example, timber sales must involve the analysis of impacts on watersheds, wildlife, recreation, and other issues.) But several factors distort the final result.

First, the proposed budget is passed on to the Secretary of Agriculture and to the Office of Management and Budget, which alter it to reflect the administration's political concerns. Throughout the 1980s and early 1990s, the administration's main concern was commodity production. With a mandate to review budgets for short-term economic impacts and for consistency with administration economic policies, OMB emphasized commodity production in final administration requests.

Second, Congress requires the Forest Service to divide its budget into 50 to 60 line items, grouped into several program areas. Timber management is thus addressed as one separate issue and wildlife or recreation as another. Naturally, budget negotiators lose sight of the interrelatedness of the many separate budget items. (Sample, 1992)

Finally, over the past decade, Congress has ignored the timber harvest levels proposed through the Forest Service planning process, instead focussing narrowly on the volume of timber to be offered for sale (timber sale targets) and on the funding needed to facilitate the timber harvest (road construction, timber sale preparation, etc). (Sample, 1992) Non-commodity resources get short shrift. In general, over the past decade timber appropriations have often been higher than those requested, while non-timber programs have usually been reduced.

Because Congress has strong constituencies arguing for heavy harvests on federal lands and strong constituencies arguing against, its policies often send conflicting directives. As Gregg (1992) observes, "…even as the legislators were busy enacting laws like the Wilderness Act, Endangered Species Act, and National Forest Planning Act, in their annual budget hearings they were forcing higher allowable cuts than forest supervisors knew were sustainable."

Influencing the Political Process

The contradictions in federal forest policy have been perpetuated by the powerful influence in Congress of the chief beneficiaries of those policies and by the commodity orientation of the Reagan and Bush administrations. At the same time, significant forest policy reforms have lacked powerful political sponsors in the Northwest and in the capital, at least until 1992 when conservation-minded candidates were elected to office in the White House and in the Northwest's congressional delegation.

Millions of dollars have been waged by timber industry groups on a Congressional fight to determine the fate of the Northwest's old-growth forests. Federal Election Commission (FEC) campaign contribution data for the period between January 1, 1985 and June 30, 1992 indicate that forest industry groups contributed nearly $5 million to hundreds of Congressional candidates. (NLMP, 1993) Although these political action committee (PAC) contributions represent a small fraction of the hundreds of millions spent on Congressional campaigns during this period, they were at least three times greater than environmental PAC contributions ($1.6 million) to all environmental causes combined, and most of the contributions were for $1,000 or more.[23] (NLMP, 1993)

Congressional candidates in Oregon and Washington gained handsomely from timber-industry PAC contributions. While the delegation from the two states holds only 3 percent of the seats in Congress, candidates for those seats received nearly 15 percent of timber industry PAC money between 1985 and 1992. (NLMP, 1993)

And the timber industry out-spent environmental PACs by more than six to one on Congressional races in the two states. Timber industry political activities at the state level have also been aimed at influencing federal policies. In 1992, a dozen timber companies bankrolled two unsuccessful efforts to recall Oregon's Governor Barbara Roberts because she refused to endorse the exemption of some timber sales from the 1991 federal court injunction prohibiting logging in spotted owl habitat on public lands. (Walth, 1992)

For twelve years before the 1992 election, the White House and executive agencies had been controlled by administrations with little enthusiasm for conservation. In 1981, the newly-elected President Reagan appointed John Crowell as assistant secretary of agriculture overseeing the U.S. Forest Service. When he was tapped, Crowell was general counsel for Louisiana Pacific—one of the largest purchasers of Forest Service timber and a company with a particularly poor environmental reputation. Working outside the established RPA planning process, Crowell pressured the Forest Service to propose as one option, sales targets of up to 16 billion boardfeet nationwide by 1990—45 percent higher than 1985 levels. Crowell then directed the Chief of the U.S. Forest Service to prepare a program that would increase harvests to 20 billion boardfeet by 2030—far higher than any of the alternatives prepared by the Forest Service during the 1985 RPA process. (CHEC, 1985) Crowell's hope was to widen the range of timber targets so that other options with high timber harvest levels would appear moderate. Ultimately, Crowell went too far, alienating both the Forest Service bureaucracy and Congress, and he resigned in 1985.

Crowell's departure, however, did nothing to dampen the Reagan and the Bush administrations' plans to keep timber harvest levels high. His successor vowed to continue policies Crowell set, and timber sales in the Northwest grew during the late 1980s. When the crisis over the northern spotted owl erupted during those years, the Bush administration sought to amend the Endangered Species Act to minimize the impacts of owl conservation on the logging industry.

Members of Congress also leaned heavily on the Bush administration and the Forest Service to keep harvest levels high. In 1991, John Mumma, Regional Forester for the Northern Region (Idaho, Montana, and the Dakotas) was transferred to a desk job in Washington when several western Republican senators and congressmen complained to the Bush Administration that timber targets were not being met. (*Washington Post*, 1991) According to Mumma, who retired rather than accept reassignment, it was impossible to meet cutting quotas and still comply with NEPA, MUSY, NFMA, and other federal laws. But no law says that the timber target must be met, and environmentalists claim Mumma fell victim to political pressures on Secretary of Agriculture Edward Madigan.

In 1993, shortly after taking office, the Clinton administration moved to resolve the logjam over forest management in the Northwest. In April 1993, President Clinton convened a "forest summit" in Portland, Oregon to discuss forest management-issues in the Pacific Northwest. Joined by Vice President Gore and six cabinet members, the president listened as loggers, environmentalists, and community leaders outlined their views on resolving the deadlock over logging in the region's dwindling old-growth forests. Although Clinton stated that the solution would have to address the needs of both endangered species and communities long dependent on logging, he indicated that changes in how forestry is practiced in the region are inevitable. He promised to develop a plan to address the "crisis" within 60 days, and within a week a federal task force was convened in Portland to begin outlining the plan. In late July, President Clinton submitted a plan to the federal courts. *(See Box 4.6.)*

Despite the change in executive branch attitudes toward the use of federal lands, the policy process in Washington, ever vulnerable to the influence of special interests, will continue to pose obstacles to forest policy reform. Shortly after the administration proposed ending subsidized commodity production on federal lands to help reduce the deficit, several western senators with substantial mining, grazing, and logging interests

at home successfully pressured the administration to drop the proposals from the economic package. While the administration has promised to pursue these proposals separately, surviving passage through committees dominated by the political allies of logging interests or weathering the threat of filibusters in the Senate will be politically difficult at best. As Rivlin (1993) points out, change in America is not easily embraced:

> ...the social and political system of North America, like most others, is designed to resist change. Those who are hurt by change tend to get more attention than the beneficiaries. The political system is willing to subsidize the status quo (to subsidize timber-dependent communities, for example) because that is less painful than figuring out how to manage change. The forces opposed to policy change tend to have the resources and organization to capture the political system, while the beneficiaries of change do not.

Public Participation

Public involvement in Forest Service policy-making takes place indirectly through the electoral process and more directly through the agency's planning process as mandated by NEPA, RPA, and the NFMA. In theory at least, the U.S. Forest Service's policy-making process is no doubt among the most democratic of any forest agency in the world. But considerable evidence suggests that broad public participation is not part of agency planning, partly because the complexity of the planning process works against thoughtful public participation. Also, by skirting such controversial issues as clearcutting, the planning process does not provide a public forum for deliberations on the key policy and planning issues facing the agency. (Shannon, 1990; Blahna and Yonts-Shepard, 1989)

National Forest plans provide the most structured opportunity for public participation. But, as O'Toole (1988) notes, "In practice, forest plans are so complex that real public participation is all but impossible." A forest plan can run to a thousand

Box 4.6. The Clinton Forest Plan

During the 1992 U.S. presidential campaign, the debate over how to resolve the stalemate over logging in old-growth forests became a regional campaign issue and received extensive national media coverage. While visiting sawmills during several campaign swings through Oregon and Washington, President Bush suggested that timber industry workers were in danger of becoming an "endangered species" in the wake of the Judge Dwyer decision to bar logging on most federal forest lands. He implied that the way to save the industry was to modify the Endangered Species Act, not to force the federal government to comply with existing laws. During a similar campaign trip, candidate Bill Clinton promised to convene a "summit" of timber workers, environmentalists, and industry representatives to address issues raised by the federal court orders.

Within weeks of his election, Clinton's transition staff began planning the forest summit by consulting with hundreds of grassroots environmentalists and timber organizations in the region, as well as scientists, economists, and politicians. The conference[1] was designed to give labor, timber, and environmental interests a chance to make their case to the President before his administration drafted a plan to address the Dwyer court injunction. After listening to 51 panelists[2] convey their hopes, fears, and recommendations, the President closed the conference by announcing his administration would develop a "balanced and comprehensive long-term policy" within 60 days.

Developing the plan took longer than expected, but for the next three months, a team of nearly 100 ecologists, foresters, economists, and sociologists[3] worked frenetically in a rented office in downtown Portland to develop options for managing Pacific Northwest forests in accordance with the broad principles articulated by President Clinton at the April 2 conference.[4] The Forest Ecosystem Management Assessment Team (FEMAT) team came up with ten options. (FEMAT, 1993) Most use watersheds as their primary unit of analysis, and all create reserve areas to provide habitat for species associated with late successional and old-growth forest ecosystems, enhance riparian habitat protection on federal forest lands, and specify that timber sales in the forest "matrix" between reserve areas retain at least some unlogged area and dispersed standing trees. Under all the scenarios, federal timber harvests are reduced significantly compared to levels in the recent past and those planned by the Forest Service and the BLM before the injunctions were in place.[5]

That said, the options differ significantly. The most protective, Option 1, establishes a large system (5.3 million hectares) of essentially inviolate reserves encompassing all late successional and old-growth forest, sharply restricts timber-management activities in forested areas outside reserves, and yields only 200 million boardfeet of annual timber volume—a 90-percent reduction from the record levels of the late 1980s. The least protective option (Option 7) calls for a much smaller reserve system (2.54 million hectares), allows thinning and timber salvage[6] within this area, and restricts timber-management outside of reserves much less stringently. Under this option, annual timber volume could total more than 2.5 billion boardfeet.[7]

On July 2, President Clinton announced that the administration would choose neither of these scenarios but would instead go with Option 9. Basically, Option 9 includes a 3.9-million hectare reserve system in which thinning and salvage are possible. In non-reserve forests, timber operations must leave 15 percent live tree volume in harvest areas. Option 9 also calls for 10 "adaptive management zones"[8] where local communities will have greater opportunities to influence management activities on federal forest lands. In addition, the President asked Congress to approve an economic assistance package of $1.2 billion for job retraining, watershed restoration, and economic development in rural communities.

Before Option 9 becomes the management strategy for federal forest lands in the Northwest, an Environmental Impact Statement (EIS) that conforms to NEPA requirements must be completed.[9] That process started in late July when the administration released a draft Environmental Impact Statement (USDA, 1993b) that included all 10 of the options evaluated by the FEMAT team for public comment.[10] After reviewing public comments, the administration will select a final plan. If the final plan complies with NEPA requirements and other conditions of the injunction, the Forest Service will be allowed to resume logging consistent with the new plan.

Whether or not Option 9 (or some variant) becomes the new framework for federal forest policies in the Pacific Northwest, the scope and scale of forest reforms in the region will, in all likelihood, remain unsettled. In his opening remarks to the Portland conference, the President predicted that the plan's "...outcome cannot possibly make everyone happy." If judged by the volume of public comments on the proposed actions to protect the northern spotted owl and other endangered species[11] and threats of lawsuits from both timber industry and environmental interests (*Oregonian*, 1993b), the President's prediction may have been understated.[12] In late October, the Ecological Society of America and the American Institute of Biological Sciences[13] released a joint report concluding that "...the choice of Option 9 cannot be justified on scientific grounds." (Marks, et al., 1993) At any rate, the Clinton forest plan may crumple under future court challenges unless it is modified to enhance the protection of endangered species or Congress resolves the deadlock legislatively. Whatever the fate of the Clinton forest plan, it does foreshadow major changes in U.S. forest policy—perhaps the most significant since the Pinchot era 90 years ago.

———

1. The forest "summit" was downgraded to a "conference," both to reduce expectations over the outcome and to avoid confusion with President Clinton's summit with Russian President Yeltsin in Vancouver, B.C. the following day.

2. According to St. Clair (1993), this included 21 slots for timber interests (divided between labor and industry), nine environmentalists, four salmon fisheries advocates, three local government representatives, two state government officials, six scientists, two economists, two sociologists, a vocational counselor, and the Archbishop of Seattle.

3. The team—known as the Forest Ecosystem Management Assessment Team (FEMAT)—was headed by Jack Ward Thomas, a U.S. Forest Service wildlife biologist, and Jerry Franklin, a University of Washington forest ecologist. Both men figured prominently in earlier scientific assessments (e.g., Thomas et al., 1993; Gordon et al., 1991; Thomas et al., 1990) of old-growth forests, endangered species, and forest management in the Pacific Northwest. Thomas was named Chief of the Forest Service in December 1993.

4. In his closing remarks to the Portland conference, President Clinton identified five principles that would guide the development of his administration's forest plan. First, the needs of loggers and timber communities must be addressed. Second, the health of the forest must be protected. Third, the plan must be scientifically sound and legally responsible. Fourth, a sustainable and predictable level of

(continued on next page)

timber must be provided. Fifth, the federal government must speak with one voice.

5. Not counting timber volume from potential thinning and salvage operations in reserve areas, the projected annual timber volumes under the FEMAT options range from 0.19 billion boardfeet to 1.84 billion boardfeet. The 1980-1989 average timber harvest on USFS and BLM lands was 3.8 billion boardfeet while national forest and BLM plans developed before the Dwyer injunctions projected harvests averaging 3.1 billion boardfeet during the 1990s.

6. Thinning operations are intended to allow managers to create uneven age stand structures in reserve areas now characterized by even age stands to augment existing old-growth and late successional habitats within reserves. Salvage provisions would allow managers to harvest trees heavily damaged by wind, fire, or disease, that might pose a threat to the old-growth and late successional stands in which they are located. These provisions have prompted considerable criticism from many environmental groups. They believe the Forest Service has a history of using "salvage" to justify logging in old-growth and roadless areas.

7. This would include timber volumes harvested in reserve areas due to thinning and salvage activities which would be allowed under all of the options except Option 1. Although no one knows how high timber volume levels from reserves would be, some estimates have speculated this could total as much as 1 billion boardfeet per year.

8. These zones total 0.5 million hectares.

9. Judge Dwyer's May 1991 injunction simply requires the U.S. Forest Service to prepare an Environmental Impact Statement (EIS) on its proposed actions to protect the northern spotted owl and other endangered species. Once an EIS, prepared in accordance with NEPA requirements, is submitted to the Court, the injunction will be lifted.

10. The public comment period (90 days) ended October 28, 1993.

11. In an October 29 memorandum to forest conservation activists, Jim Owens, Executive Director of the Western Ancient Forest Campaign, wrote "Our understanding is that somewhere between 80,000–100,000 comments were written on Option 9. The Forest Service...is scrambling to develop processes and capacity for what could be the largest public response to an EIS comment period in history." The Forest Service asked the court to extend the period for reviewing comments by 90 days, which means the final plan and a signed "Record of Decision" will be finished by the end of March 1994.

12. A July survey of editorial reactions to the Clinton plan by Greenwire (1993), indicated that many newspapers observed that no one was happy with the plan.

13. The Ecological Society of America (ESA) is a scientific society of 7,000 professional ecologists, and the American Institute of Biological Sciences (AIBS) is a federation of 50 scientific societies and 80,000 members.

pages or more. Typically, the language is bureaucratic, the pages of terms and definitions mind-boggling, and the scores of data tables in tiny type overwhelming. Public questions unanswered by the draft plan and referred to the agency are usually answered with references to the FORPLAN computer model, though a dozen other programs are also used. (O'Toole, 1988) Unfortunately, FORPLAN computer runs are typically two-to-three inch bundles of computer printouts filled with cryptic codes and numbers with little explanation. Public requests for the data that went into the model are often filled by providing another printout consisting entirely of numbers that have no meaning to the lay person. According to O'Toole (1988), most FORPLAN experts outside of the Forest Service work for the timber industry and "The number of citizens' groups who have been able to penetrate FORPLAN's mysteries without the help of outside consultants can be counted on one hand." With full public participation limited to forest policy junkies with formidable computer skills, interest groups on both sides of the issue have confined themselves largely to seeing which group can generate the most form letters and postcards.[24]

Other barriers to full public participation are also formidable. Blahna and Yonts-Shepard (1989) studied the development of thirteen National Forest plans and identified three barriers besides the complex, technocratic nature of the agency's planning process. First, public participation in the planning process is highly selective. Most National Forests took a passive approach to soliciting public involvement in planning: in the early stages of planning, public comments averaged fewer than 140 per forest and virtually all came from commodity-oriented users of the forest resources. (Blahna and Yonts-Shepard, 1989) After the release of the draft plan, forests averaged over 840 written public comments from local, regional, and national interests, most of which emphasized conservation and were highly critical of the draft plan.

Second, as Blahna and Yonts-Shepard found, forest planners rarely interacted with the public mid-course in planning, when key decisions are made. After years of work and debate,[25] many forest staff members involved in planning were too attached to their own ideas to throw the planning process wide open. Of the thirteen National Forests studied, only one (Green Mountain National Forest in Vermont) encouraged public participation throughout the planning cycle and held interactive meetings on high-conflict issues during this period. In the end, it was one of the few National Forest plans that was not appealed—and the only one amongst the thirteen studied.

Third, most National Forest plans met the minimum legal requirements for public participation by using the least confrontational methods possible. Typically, written or one-way communication was encouraged instead of direct interaction.[26] Acting in isolation, public interest groups had to develop their own vision of what the plans should include, and some took extreme stands just to carve out unclaimed political territory. In other cases, contentious issues identified by the public early in the planning process had been sanitized or buried by agency decision-makers in the draft plans finally released, forcing the public to resolve their disputes in court. As Blahna and Yonts-Shepard (1989) conclude, controversies over forest plans stem mostly from the Forest Service's attempts to avoid confrontation.

Structural Ignorance

As in Indonesia, the political discourse on forest policies in the United States is riddled with unproven or even false assumptions that help preserve the *status quo*. Those with huge stakes in current policies often believe these assumptions. In other cases, the assumptions are calculated half-truths devised to convince enough voters and policy-makers that forest policy reforms threaten their self-interest or that current forest policies and practices are adequate.

In the United States, one of the most questionable assumptions promoted by the timber industry and public land-management agencies is that federal timber is needed to meet an ever-growing demand for wood fiber. Since the U.S. Forest Service was founded in 1905, it has consistently predicted that demands for its timber would continue to rise and that timber supplies would be in short supply. (OTA, 1990) In the 1989 RPA assessment, the agency predicted that total demand for wood fiber will increase by 50 percent over the next five decades. (USDA, 1989) To meet that demand, the agency assumes, harvest levels in the National Forests will have to increase by 20 percent, and even then prices in real terms will increase by as much as 12 percent each decade.

If history is any guide, these assumptions are likely to prove incorrect. The agency's own statistics show that U.S. demand for timber has actually declined by nearly 50 percent since the turn of the century, although it has increased by 0.3–0.4 percent annually in recent decades (MacCleery, 1991)—considerably less than the 1 percent annual growth forecast by the 1989 RPA assessment. Meanwhile, the net volume of timber on private timberlands in the United States increased by over 40 percent between 1952 and 1987. (Waddell et al., 1989) Even for softwoods (the major timber type harvested in National Forests), private timberland stocks increased significantly—by 22 percent between 1952 and 1987.

Some proponents of continued harvests of Pacific Northwest old-growth argue in response to such evidence that this timber is needed for high-quality construction lumber and specialty products, such as furniture and musical instruments. But this justification, especially for construction lumber, is increasingly out of step with the times: technological advances have produced oriented-strand board, chipboard, finger-joint board, particle board, and a host of other emerging composite wood products that can be made from a wide variety of wood types that are abundant on private timberlands. And nothing close to one billion boardfeet of old-growth timber is required to satisfy the annual demand for fine furniture and musical instruments (tens of millions of boardfeet are more likely).

Relying on such unproven assumptions contributes to poor forest management decisions that can have irreversible consequences. As O'Toole (1988) notes, excessive road-building is a case in point:

> [Long-term economic forecasting] trends often lead planners to take irreversible actions—such as proposing to build roads in roadless areas or to invade the habitat of endangered species—that would not have been proposed if trends were not used…. The decision not to build roads is completely reversible: The Forest Service can build roads to harvest the timber at any time. If future

timber prices increase relative to road costs and recreation values, the roadless area may be able to contribute to next year's timber supply. In the meantime, there is no need to second-guess the future and foreclose options by building roads today.

Another common assumption is that, even if subsidized public timber sales lose money, they contribute to "community stability"—jobs, income, profits, and economic development. Although Chapter III showed how important timber can be to some rural economies in the Pacific Northwest, timber dependency is not synonymous with community stability. As noted, timber employment declined even as harvests increased to record levels during the 1980s due to automation, log exports, and regional shifts in timber industry investments. Although many small sawmills survived (at least until 1991) thanks to the availability of public old-growth timber, larger forces have doomed most of them whether the last old-growth forests are logged or not.

In any case, old-growth timber has already disappeared from many areas and would run out within the next two decades if harvests at 1980s levels continued. What will communities depend on for development then? The timber industry will be gone, property values will be down, and the recreational potential that could attract investment and diversify the local economy will be greatly diminished. Knize (1991) suggests that the mythical link between National Forest timber sales and community stability has created destructive dependencies that have foreclosed future options:

> The loggers and mill workers who depend on National Forest timber are, like the forests, victims of federal policy. Since the end of World War II, the Forest Service has fostered in their communities an expectation that federal timber would be available indefinitely, and a way of life has evolved around that expectation. If the Forest Service and the loggers' elected representatives had been honest with their constituents even ten years ago, and warned them that

the supply of trees could not support their industry forever, mill owners and loggers might not have invested further in lumber operations that are doomed, National Forest timber or no. These communities were misled, and they deserve aid in adjusting to what is for them a catastrophe.

OTA (1992) further notes that payments to counties based on federal timber receipts actually destabilizes communities since such payments swing widely from year to year due to economic and market fluctuations even if the harvest isn't restricted. What's needed for stability, OTA states, is "Fair and consistent compensation for the tax exempt status of National Forest lands and activities [that] could stabilize county payments, regardless of how the lands are managed."

Other questionable assumptions will emerge as economic, social, and political conditions change. The overriding point here is that policy-making based on myths can't succeed except by accident.

Toward Effective Forest Policy-making

Recent attempts to deal with forest problems internationally, through the Tropical Forestry Action Plan and the International Tropical Timber Organization in the 1980s and, more recently, through attempts to negotiate an international forest convention prior to the Rio Summit, have foundered for want of national-level commitment to policy reform. But before any such commitments can solidify, fundamental structural weaknesses and failures in the policy-making process itself—whether in wealthy industrialized countries such as the United States or in developing countries such as Indonesia—have to be addressed.

Four basic issues bedevil forest policy-making in both the United States and Indonesia. First, planning, legislative, and regulatory mechanisms are overly complex, incoherent, and therefore do not function very well. Second, the aggregate

body of plans, laws, and regulations emerging from this system is so arcane and impenetrable that only insiders and powerful interests with specialized knowledge and contacts can manipulate it. Third, mechanisms and opportunities for informed and sustained participation in forest policy-making are inadequate. Many stakeholders, particularly those who are not wealthy or politically connected are simply frozen out of the process. A lack of public access to useful and timely information upon which to base participation exacerbates the problem. Fourth, forestry policy-making processes are characterized by a jurisdictional and intellectual "sectoralism" which frustrates development of policies based on an integrated view of economic activity within and outside forest areas, much less a view that takes into full account the considerable social impacts of forest policies.

If national governments and their citizens—and the people of the planet as a whole—are to slow forest loss and put forest management on a sustainable and equitable footing, these issues must be confronted with as complete and objective a picture as possible of the problems to be faced, the costs and benefits of alternative responses, and the distribution of those costs and benefits. Fearless and informed dialogue is thus the first step toward addressing the systemic political weaknesses that have stymied forest policy reforms. Once these weaknesses are corrected, hard choices about how to break the economics of inertia and the stranglehold of current forest-tenure regimes will remain, but so will hope that we can manage our forests sustainably and equitably into the next century and beyond.

Notes

1. In September 1992, for example, P.T. Indah Kiat, the country's largest pulp and paper producer, was forced to apologize in parliament for hiring almost 700 workers from China. While there is a large expatriate community working in Indonesia, "In fact the main cause of the problem is not the number of foreign workers itself, but more their country of origin and the ethnic origin

[Chinese] of the project owners", said Defense Minister Benny Murdani in his remarks to Parliament on the matter. (Aznam, 1992a)

2. Law No. 8/1985 Concerning Societal Organizations.

3. As noted in a recent court decision (*Seattle Audubon Society v. Moseley*, 1992), the laws governing the National Forests make them the only opportunity to manage for all forest values: "Management of the National Forests in compliance with the National Forest Management Act is vital because other measures are inadequate for many species.... [For example] the efforts of the Fish and Wildlife Service fall short of systematic management of a biological community. In this sense the National Forests offer a last chance."

4. The public can indirectly influence forest policy and planning for private land through state forest practices legislation and such policy mechanisms as state forestry commissions or boards (which, in general, are dominated by private forest land owners).

5. *Perkins v. Bergland* (1979), 608F. 2d 803, 806 (U.S. Ninth Circuit Court of Appeals).

6. Actually, the RPA planning process starts with an analytical "assessment" of the current forest situation. Inventories of forest data and trends are carried out every ten years. The "program" to implement strategic responses to the assessment is updated every five years, as is the "statement of policy," which is supposed to provide budget guidance and programmatic commitment to the strategic directions outlined in the "program." Finally, on an annual basis, the Forest Service is to provide Congress with an annual budget that reflects the priorities of the "program" and "policy statement" and an annual report on progress in implementing the "program."

7. The National Forest Management Act also forces the agency to satisfy other federal environmental laws, such as the National Environmental Protection Act (NEPA), that require the federal government to evaluate the environmental impact of its actions and to explicitly consider the impact of management activities on endangered species.

8. Provision 6 (k) of the National Forest Management Act.

9. *Northern Spotted Owl v. Hodel* (1988); *Northern Spotted Owl v. Lujan* (1991); *Marbled Murrelet v. Lujan* (1992).

10. *Seattle Audubon Society v. Evans* (1987); *Seattle Audubon Society v. Evans* (1991); *Seattle Audubon Society v. Mosely* (1992).

11. *Lane County Audubon Society v. Jamison* (1991); *Portland Audubon Society v. Lujan* (1992).

12. All appeals of these federal district court rulings were rejected by the Ninth Circuit Court of Appeals.

13. The Forest Service does not consider road construction costs a subsidy since they claim the roads generate non-timber benefits as well. For example, logging roads are justified on the basis of providing better recreational access and fire control, and facilitating the agency's efforts to manage a wide range of forest resources. (O'Toole, 1988) However, during planning, the presumed beneficiaries of these roads, including outdoor recreational users, state Fish and Game agencies, and others often vehemently oppose road construction. (Repetto et al., 1992) Moreover, many logging roads are slated for removal after loggers no longer need them.

14. Flora (1990) estimates that there is an average $200 differential between upper-grade logs sold domestically and those exported.

15. A 1990 federal law that phased out exports of logs from state lands was overturned by the 9th Federal Circuit Court of Appeals in May 1993. Several Washington state agencies had brought the lawsuit claiming that the state government would lose nearly $500 million in timber sales through the 1990s and thus "cripple its ability to

adequately fund public education." (*Wall Street Journal*, 1993)

16. Most other countries restrict or prohibit raw-log exports.

17. Exports can generate far more profits than domestic processing since relatively few capital, labor, and other processing costs are involved. Exports are especially attractive because of the overall declining international competitiveness of forest manufacturing in the Pacific Northwest.

18. Approximately 500 million boardfeet came from Washington State lands. (USFS/BLM, 1990)

19. In 1991, 84 percent of agency revenues came from timber receipts, six percent from minerals, six percent from recreation, one percent from grazing, and three percent from "other" sources. (OMB, 1992)

20. The project budget is for such on-the-ground activities as timber sales, road construction, campground maintenance, wildlife management, and other activities, and totals approximately 60 percent of the total Forest Service Budget. This excludes the administration or overhead budget, which usually amounts to 40 percent of the total congressional appropriation.

21. This assumes that there were no efforts to eliminate below-cost timber sales or to raise recreation and other user fees.

22. When Congress sets the annual timber-production targets, they reflect the end result of the complex planning process carried out by the Forest Service under RPA and NFMA, as well as negotiations between Congress and the Executive Branch.

23. The legal limit for PAC contributions to an individual candidate is $5,000 per election.

24. According to O'Toole (1988), on many plans, over 80 percent of the public comments are made in form letters or form postcards.

25. National forest plans typically take from six to eight years to develop.

26. According to Blahna and Yonts-Shepard (1989), the U.S. Forest Service spent 96 percent of its public affairs budget on "one-way" information programs such as the Smokey the Bear, Woodsy Owl, news releases and speeches, and brochures and audiovisual presentations. Only 4 percent of the budget was spent on trying to determine public opinion on policy and planning issues, and most of this was merely to solicit and code written comments from the public.

V. Conclusions and Recommendations

nalysis of the root causes of the forest crises in Indonesia and the United States indicates that effective policies to protect forests' ecological integrity, make production of diverse forest products and services sustainable and equitable, allow for management at a socially workable scale, and ensure broad participation in forest decision-making can be made only after these structural issues are addressed. Here we provide some recommendations for action in Indonesia and the United States that directly address these issues.

Of course, generic policy recommendations must be put into perspective. As Raikes notes, it is

> ...difficult to say what are practical suggestions, when one's research tends to show that what is politically feasible is usually too minor to make any difference, while changes significant enough to be worthwhile are often unthinkable in practical political terms. In any case, genuine practicality in making policy suggestions requires detailed knowledge of a particular country or area; its history, culture, vegetation, existing situation, and much more besides. Lists of general "policy conclusions" make it all too easy for the rigid-minded to apply them as general recipes, without thought, criticism, or adjustment for circumstances. (Raikes 1988)

Yet, much in the experiences of Indonesia and the United States is relevant in other countries,

provided that adjustments for particular circumstances are made thoughtfully and critically.

Reforming Forest Policy-making

Changes in the process by which forest policy issues are framed and discussed, and policy decisions are made, are a prerequisite for changing anything else.

In Indonesia, the following steps need to be taken to address structural deficiencies in forest policy-making:

- *Give high-level political recognition to the legitimacy of participation by all actors and interests affected by or involved in forest policy.* In Indonesia, government at the presidential and ministerial level must formally acknowledge, through word and deed, that the national government is not and should not be the only legitimate arbiter of forest policy; rather, local communities, non-governmental organizations, and the private business sector must be formally recognized as actors who—like timber companies—are already key players, or who —like NGOs and forest dwellers—have a legitimate right to be. Some encouraging developments are the 1992 recognition by law of the territorial rights of indigenous forest communities *(see Chapter II)*, the increasing receptivity of many government agencies to working with NGOs in exercises such as formulation of the 1991 National Biodiversity Action Plan, and the increasingly public debate within government on the extent and propriety of timber companies' role in policy-making.

- *Increase public access to information relevant to forest policy decision-making.* The policy process can never truly serve and benefit from the full range of affected interests and actors unless all parties receive relevant information in a useful form and at the right time. This is still an extremely grave problem in Indonesia, where most information is held closely by forestry officials, local communities are generally kept in the dark about projects and policies that will drastically affect their lives until it is too late for them to influence the course of events, and NGOs must rely on leaks from sympathetic officials to figure out what is going on. On the other hand, the national media is far more diverse and outspoken than it was even a few years ago, and many publications now routinely report on environmental issues. The proliferation of computers and fax machines allows even small NGOs and individuals to link into a global network of information sources. Recently initiated donor-aided forest and conservation projects, such as the World Bank-assisted Global Environment Facility (GEF) project in Sumatra have broken new ground: with government's consent, NGOs and local communities will receive full documentation on project preparation at the earliest stages. Needed now is a bold commitment by the government to institutionalized, legally-guaranteed freedom of information in all of its forestry activities and policy processes.

- *Initiate pilot efforts to manage forests regionally, integrating different sectors.* Experience shows that most forests can be managed and conserved successfully in Indonesia only through a cross-sectoral, landscape-scale approach that integrates diverse forest uses and takes surrounding social and economic needs and realities into account. The first step in what must be a long term-strategy is to initiate more strategic pilot efforts, like those supported by the Asian Development Bank, GEF, and other donors. The government, donors, and NGOs should continue to support and should also evaluate such pilot efforts, correcting mis-steps as the initiatives mature. In the longer term, the government must draw on this experience to come up with ways to institutionalize the cross-sectoral, landscape-scale approach to forest management within its agencies.

- *Remove obstacles to the empowerment and participation of weak and disenfranchised groups with a stake in forest policy and build these groups' capacity to participate.* Indonesia's government recognizes that its considerable development successes over the past several decades have left some groups and areas behind, and it has made the eradication of poverty its highest priority in the current Five-Year Development Plan. Moreover, many in government are beginning to realize that economic development makes political development inevitable. In forest policy, the government has repeatedly noted the importance of "popular participation." But giving this phrase practical meaning will require loosening restrictions on the freedom of forest-dwellers, NGOs, and others to form organizations, to hold meetings, to speak out in the media, and to contact like-minded groups around the country and the world. Government should also provide resources and political support to strengthen the capacity of local and national NGOs—indispensable intermediaries between policy-makers and local communities. Finally, if local communities are to become true partners in managing portions of the nation's forest estate, laws must change to allow community-based forest-management groups to establish a legal corporate identity that allows these groups to make decisions democratically on their own and to possess and manage land and capital.

In the United States, overcoming structural problems in forest policy-making will require the following steps:

- *Develop a new alliance of all who stand to benefit from forest policy reform.* The constituency promoting forest policy reforms has swelled during the past decade. Scientists, resource economists, natural resource managers (including foresters), and sometimes even fiscal conservatives, have joined environmentalists in calling for reform. Still, most pro-reform coalitions represent but a small segment of those who would benefit from change. The potential alliance should thus be expanded to include urban residents who enjoy water and recreation benefits, commercial and recreational fishermen who need aquatic habitat protected, small town and rural residents seeking stable economies and greater political and economic access, private land owners who could profit as forest resource values rise, and forest industry innovators and entrepreneurs looking for business opportunities. Proponents of change should start to expand the active constituency for reforms by first analyzing who stands to gain from reform and why. Through such techniques as "participatory rural appraisal," forest-based communities should also be involved in the analysis of forest resource problems and opportunities. Although it cannot substitute for analysis, dialogue is also critical to expanding the alliance of interests supporting forest policy reform. While the Clinton forest conference in April 1993 was a symbolic step in that direction, reformers should encourage a sustained dialogue on forest policy issues with all stakeholders, especially at local levels.

- *Improve participation in forest planning and policy development so the public gets more involved in defining what Americans want from their forests.* Although sophisticated by the standards of most countries, mechanisms for public participation in forest planning and policy-making do not encourage broad involvement in determining "desired future conditions" in public forests or in monitoring the Forest Service's performance. To make amends, the Forest Service should actively solicit all stakeholders to help develop National Forest plans; involve the public in the development of forest-management options from beginning to end; keep the public informed of controversial forest-management issues; and compile and distribute policy-relevant data to the public and their elected representatives. Since a growing number of national and local NGOs are analyzing critical forest-management issues, forest-management agencies have an extra incentive to involve the public more—avoiding costly and lengthy legal conflicts.

- *Give scientists and professional natural resource managers more say in determining what resource-use levels are sustainable.* Despite the increasing diversification of professionals (e.g., ecologists, sociologists, wildlife biologists, hydrologists, etc.) in natural resource management agencies, science and professional judgment are often subordinated to political considerations to maximize commodity production. The annual timber targets that Congress set, for instance, become the benchmarks for measuring agency performance, in turn creating pressures for managers to sacrifice forest resources against the better judgment of agency scientists and resource professionals. Recent announcements by the U.S. Forest Service and the Bureau of Land Management that they are adopting "ecosystem management" policies suggests that science will soon play a greater role in future management decisions. But advocates of forest policy reform should step up the pace of change by working with forest management agencies to define "forest ecosystem management" policies, setting benchmarks or standards for monitoring progress in ecosystem management, and developing legal and administrative measures that reward progress toward ecosystem management goals. At the same time, perverse incentives that currently

101

reward environmentally and economically unsustainable actions must be eliminated.

- *Initiate pilot efforts to manage forests regionally, integrating the needs of different sectors and landowners.* Consistent with experiences in other countries, it is becoming increasingly apparent that U.S. forests can be managed and conserved successfully only through a cross-sectoral, regional approach that integrates diverse forest uses and takes full account of surrounding social and economic needs and realities. A number of recent innovative proposals reflect this approach, including efforts in the "Greater Yellowstone Ecosystem" of Wyoming, Idaho, and Montana and the forest lands of northern New England. So far, the federal government—a major landowner with the power to provide technical assistance, tax incentives, data, and other critical resources—has shied away from a leadership role in these efforts. On the other hand, the new administration appears willing to experiment with landscape ecosystem approaches to the management of natural resources in other settings, in part to head off costly and divisive conflicts over endangered species.

Toward Sustainable Forest Economies

Forest economies in both Indonesia and the United States are driven by commodity-production policies that concentrate economic benefits within certain groups while shifting costs to the wider public. Policies that support a transition to more sustainable forest economies will be crucial to the future of natural forests in both countries.

In Indonesia, the following steps will promote the transition to sustainable forest economies:

- *Conduct comprehensive forest inventories and utilize natural resources accounting methods to determine the real status and trends of the resource base and the full values of alternative uses.* Rational economic choices in the forestry sector cannot be made without a full accounting of what the resource base is and what the real costs and benefits of alternative uses are. Both private and government-sponsored inventory and mapping efforts are under way, promising a far better picture of the resource base by the mid-1990s. Necessary too, however, is a shift in the ways that the costs and benefits of alternative policies are accounted for. In particular, economic-assessment methods should be developed that account for the values of non-timber forest products, of local forest products and services that do not enter formal markets, and of such "ecosystem services" as the maintenance of hydrological functions and the prevention of erosion and landslides. Some preliminary theoretical work has been done (Repetto, et. al, 1989), but government and the private sector have yet to internalize the natural resources accounting approach systematically.

- *Account fully and publicly for the economic, ecological, and social costs and benefits of forest exploitation.* Just as important as detailing what the true costs and benefits of alternative policy choices are is detailing exactly who gains and who loses. While government agencies can facilitate this kind of "distributional analysis" by freeing up access to relevant information, much of this work is likely to be done by researchers and NGOs and injected into public debate by the press. The growing capacity and willingness of independent researchers to take on questions of equity in the forestry sector is documented by the many studies cited in this report, and the increasing freedom of the press to report on sensitive forest controversies strengthens this movement. To give it added momentum, aid donors should support the development of independent research capacity.

- *Eliminate policies that lead to resource waste or that subsidize special interests at the expense of the public.* While the government is beginning to reform timber-concessions, waste still pervades the system. A significant example is the way timber levies are calculated for plywood: it is assumed that two cubic meters of logs are used to make one of plywood, but nobody checks to see if that much is actually used, so the incentive is not to use raw material efficiently. A number of other perverse incentives bear scrutiny as well, including the still-low level of government rent capture from logging operations, and the generous subsidies granted for establishing industrial timber plantations.

- *Promote sustainable forest uses and provide incentives for forest conservation.* While timber production will remain the cornerstone of Indonesia's forestry sector, the same amount of revenue could be realized from a lower level of timber harvest if non-timber uses received greater emphasis. Nature tourism, the sustainable exploitation of non-timber forest products, and "biodiversity prospecting" for commercially valuable genetic resources all warrant proportionately greater attention.

In the United States, a transition to more sustainable forest economies will require the following steps:

- *Use natural resource accounting methods to determine the true status of the resource base, the trends affecting it, and the full values of alternative uses.* Even though the Forest Service and other land-management agencies have collected voluminous data on forest resources, serious gaps exist in the information they gather and monitor.

- *Eliminate below-cost timber sales and other policies that invite waste or subsidize special interests at the expense of the public.* Much U.S. Forest Service land is unsuitable for commercial timber production, especially in the Intermountain West, Alaska, and the East. Yet, timber targets set by Congress and pressure from local timber interests have perpetuated timber operations in such areas—despite National Forest Management Act directives to remove these areas from

the timber base. Although the subsidy implicit in below-cost timber sales varies with the volume and price of timber sold, in recent years it has been estimated at up to $400 million annually. Such sales damage other resources (fisheries, recreation, water quality, and wildlife habitat) worth more to the public than timber in areas where below-cost sales are prevalent. Requiring the Forest Service to establish a minimum bid for all timber sales so as to recover the full costs of growing and selling trees (and protecting valuable non-timber assets) would do much to eliminate these subsidies. Although below-cost timber sales are uncommon in the Pacific Northwest (especially in National Forests west of the Cascades), other policies create subsidies in conflict with the public interest. Tax credits for the export of raw logs save Northwest log producers nearly $100 million annually, according to the Congressional Joint Committee on Taxation. At the same time, road-construction credits against timber purchases that amount to interest-free loans, form an indirect public subsidy to logging in the Northwest that makes harvesting on public lands more attractive than purchasing private timber supplies.

- *Invest the savings from the elimination of public subsidies to private timber interests in the restoration of degraded forest lands and the economic diversification of communities that have grown dependent on federal timber resources.* Valuable forest assets—among them, fisheries, habitat for wildlife and biodiversity, and forested watersheds—throughout the United States have been damaged by forest practices, many of which were encouraged by federal subsidies. Investing the savings gained by eliminating such subsidies would increase the forest's future values and economic returns and give local forest economies a new lease on life.

- *Replace federal programs for sharing revenues from timber sales with fair and consistent compensation to counties that have tax-exempt federal forest lands in their jurisdictions.* Counties with extensive federal forest lands have come to depend on federal forest revenues (90 percent of them from timber) to fund schools, roads, and social services. Naturally, local government support for perpetuating timber sales is fierce even in the face of growing damage to other important resources and industries. Yet, even continued revenues from sales would not mean stability for forest communities: timber revenue shares to counties can fluctuate by as much as 50 percent or more from year to year.

Congress should require a study to determine appropriate compensation methods and levels and then replace the current system with stable tax-equivalency payments, regardless of how the lands are managed. Alternatively, federal payments could be based on net rather than gross revenues, provided that the federal government captures more revenue from valuable non-timber resources, such as recreation, than it currently does. Under this alternative approach, local governments would encourage the efficient management of federal lands for their most valued uses. But because many important forest assets and functions (e.g., biodiversity, water quality) are unlikely to ever be adequately recognized in forest revenues and user fees, fixed compensation rates per unit area are probably preferable.

- *Encourage the development of markets for sustainably produced forest products, including timber, recreation, wildlife and fisheries, watershed protection, and such other non-timber resources as biodiversity.* Although some timber-dominated local economies will move heavily into service, professional, and trade activities, many communities in the Northwest (and in other parts of the country) will always be dependent on forest resources. Sustainable forest economies will thus depend on building markets for more sustainably produced forest products. Many such products will be produced by small,

entrepreneurial businesses without much investment capital or easy access to markets. The private sector, which must take the lead, can work with non-profit organizations to help build such markets by educating the public on the benefits and quality of forest products created without destroying forest diversity and productivity and on the impacts of buying products whose prices don't include the cost of externalities.

In partnership with Southshore Bank, (which pioneered community-based banking to fund locally initiated urban redevelopment in Chicago), a Portland-based non-governmental organization, Ecotrust, is exploring options to create community-based financing for small businesses that do not have negative environmental impacts in rural forest areas. (Ecotrust, 1992) To facilitate such important private initiatives, governments should back private investors in sustainable forest activities with loan guarantees or revolving low-interest loans and target investment tax credits for more environmentally sustainable businesses.

- *Establish incentives to encourage private investment in sustainable timber management on commercial timber lands and small tracts of non-commercial lands.* The Pacific Northwest will remain an important source of timber for the rest of the country and internationally, even as public timber supplies contract and the forest products industry's regional economic role shrinks compared to those of services. But on many privately owned forest lands, productivity is not as high as it could be and non-timber benefits are limited.

Where timberland values and timber prices availability are not high enough to encourage more investment in currently unproductive private forest lands, tax credits and other incentives to encourage the restoration of forest productivity should be considered. On all private forest lands, state and federal policies can encourage resource management that leads to a wider array of public forest benefits by offering tax and other fiscal incentives tied to enhanced water quality, wildlife habitat, and other forest-related assets and functions for which land-owners are not traditionally paid. Finally, temporary targeted investment tax credits could be offered to smaller producers dependent on old-growth timber so they can retool to handle second- and third-growth processing. Similar incentives could be offered to processors to invest in capital improvements to produce high-quality processed and finished wood products for the specifications of the demanding international market. Meanwhile, the United States should negotiate lower foreign trade barriers to finished wood products and eliminate tax incentives for the export of raw logs and minimally processed wood products.

Revamping Forest-Tenure Regimes

> Forest ecosystems will be managed sustainably only when it is in the best interest of forest users and managers. In both Indonesia and the United States, rights to and responsibilities for using forest resources are often defined and distributed in ways that do not encourage sustainable management.

In Indonesia, steps to correct deficiencies in forest tenure regimes to promote sustainable forest management will include the following:

- *Conduct a Ministerial-level legal and regulatory review of the status of customary **adat** lands in forest areas and produce a coherent and authoritative statement of law and policy based on the recognition that legitimate customary land rights are valid under national law and asserting that their protection is in the national interest.* While many government- and NGO-sponsored pilot projects are currently trying to get *adat* forest land rights recognized in the context of sustainable and productive forest-management systems, they are likely to remain isolated demonstration projects unless government launches a "top-down" effort to clarify

the status of *adat* rights and makes sense of the confusing tangle of laws and regulations currently governing forest tenure.

- *Determine, map, and accord recognized legal status to the ancestral territories of rural peoples living in or next to public forest lands.* Once the government recognizes *adat* rights, the hard work of translating a commitment into practice remains. Conflicts and differing interpretations are inevitable, and not every *adat* right will be compatible with new sustainable forest-management strategies. But secure boundaries for both the nation's forests and the communities that live in them or on their fringes are essential preconditions for making new strategies work.

- *Strictly enforce laws requiring recipients of logging-concession rights to care for the land, levying heavy fines and revoking licenses as necessary.* The government has already begun to crack down on some concession-holders, but it does not have the information or the inspection capacity needed to do the job right. Establishing an independent inspection capacity and requiring a stiff "performance bond" from concession-holders would go a long way toward bringing errant logging firms into compliance with their concession agreements.

- *Review and eliminate overlaps between timber concessions and protected areas.* Given the national and global significance of Indonesia's biodiversity, eliminating logging activities in protected areas and in areas immediately adjacent to them must be a high priority for government if it is to make good on its strong commitment to conserving biodiversity. Given the timber industry's economic importance and political strength, government will not be able to eliminate these concessions by fiat, any more than the U.S. Government has been able to halt logging in the remaining old-growth forests in the Pacific Northwest. Needed is a negotiating approach based on an understanding of the costs that concession-holders will have to bear and of the need to at least partly compensate them, perhaps with other concession areas or preferential rights to develop industrial timber plantations. International donors should support such efforts, given the global interest in conserving Indonesia's biodiversity.

- *Establish a category of forest property right that allows certain qualifying logged concessions to become "community concessions" restored and managed by local communities with help from government agencies and the private sector.* Many logged-over forests in Indonesia could be restored if access could be controlled. Local communities are, in many cases, the parties best situated to control access, provided they have an incentive to keep the area forested. Pilot efforts of this sort already under way in Kalimantan should be encouraged, improved, and expanded.

- *Strictly review and monitor those granted Industrial Timber Plantation Rights to ensure that plantations are sited only on truly degraded lands and that establishing plantations does not displace the sources of livelihood (e.g. grazing land) for local people or, if it does, that these people are consulted well in advance of any land-use change and receive just and adequate negotiated compensation.* Timber plantations will play an important part in Indonesia's forestry sector in coming decades, but they need not be allowed to destroy both natural forests and local people's livelihoods. If common sense prevailed, natural forest, even so-called "secondary" forests, would never be cleared expressly to establish plantations; instead, the millions of hectares of already degraded lands would be used. Equally important, careful socio-economic surveys should be made of all "degraded land" areas targeted for plantation development; some will certainly turn out to be important, if undocumented, resource bases for local communities, which should be party to plantation planning and siting and should have a say about what species are to be grown.

In the United States, steps to improve the balance between rights to use forest resources and responsibilities to maintain them include:

- *Strictly enforce existing responsibilities to maintain forest resources on public and private lands.* Timber companies are already required to protect some forest resources, and recent tougher laws on state forest practices in Washington state are encouraging. But such laws have been enforced selectively or lackadaisically on both public and private lands throughout the Pacific Northwest. Tightening enforcement will produce public benefits evident for years. It will save taxpayers the expense of destroyed fisheries habitat, recovering endangered species, stabilizing erosion-prone slopes, and minimizing infrastructure and personal losses due to flooding exacerbated or caused by poor forest management.

- *Identify the forest areas most important for biodiversity and other non-timber "forest values" and protect the areas where logging and non-timber values are found to be incompatible.* Given their extremely limited extent, all remaining old-growth forests on public lands should be protected from logging and other uses that would irreversibly reduce their biodiversity, and their use in scientific research, recreation, and other activities. Accordingly, efforts to expand habitat areas critical to the survival of threatened and endangered species should receive priority over commodity production. Habitat restoration should also take precedence over timber production in public forest areas where additional species are likely to fall into the Endangered Species Act listing process if remedial actions are not taken. In other unprotected and publicly owned natural forest areas not yet converted to mono-cultural forest stands, an ecological basis for natural forest management should be firmly established before any logging occurs. (Alternatively, logging should be restricted to areas already converted to highly modified or monocultural stands.) The ecological goals should be:

- protecting natural regeneration of important successional and dominant tree species by retaining biotic diversity, maintaining suitable microclimates for generation, and allowing fires and other natural disturbances that are part of natural successional processes;

- preserving nutrient cycles by protecting mineral nutrients, organic soil materials, and soil microfauna and leaving woody debris;

- protecting the forest from large-scale disturbances to which it is not adapted—in most areas, this means extensive and complete removal of tree canopies since clearcutting may give tree species (such as Douglas fir) an advantage while limiting the successional role of other trees and the tremendous biological resources associated with naturally regenerating forest ecosystems;

- and protecting contiguous natural forest areas from conversion and maintaining relatively undisturbed habitat corridors to the nearest large similar forest habitat.

- *Develop forest ecosystem management plans that anticipate conflicts between commodity-extraction and the conservation of endangered species and other non-commodity values.* Long-range trends for a wide array of forest resources need to be established through new monitoring programs so that forest managers, policy-makers, and the public can anticipate and deflect emerging problems and conflicts—whether they involve timber supply, water quality, carbon storage, habitat area, or recreational opportunities. Such information should be collected from all forest areas to give public and private forest managers the widest view of possible problems and potential solutions. Actions based on this information should ideally be determined at a scale in which forests, ecological processes, and economic activities are strongly linked. The scale may be defined by some combination of watershed boundaries, biogeographic classification, or economic markets, but preferably not by arbitrary political boundaries.

Possible actions should be developed by task forces composed of individuals representing diverse interests with a stake in area forests. This should include representatives of government agencies (local, state, and federal), private landowners and businesses with a stake in the area's forest resources as well as representatives of local communities, non-governmental organizations, and interested members of the public. Such task forces might call for voluntary actions by private and public interests, or for policy changes accomplished through tax and fiscal incentives, reform of existing laws and institutions, or new regulations.

Charles V. Barber is a Senior Associate in the Biological Resources and Institutions Program at the World Resources Institute, where he works on legal and institutional analysis of forestry and biodiversity conservation issues. Prior to joining WRI, he worked in Indonesia as a consultant for the World Bank, the Ford Foundation, and the U.N. Food and Agriculture Organization. **Nels C. Johnson** is an Associate in the Biological Resources and Institutions Program at WRI, where he works on biodiversity conservation planning and forest management policies. Previously, he worked for the International Institute for Environment and Development in Washington, the Center for International Development and Environment at WRI, and Oregon State University's cooperative forest research program. **Emmy Hafild** has spent the last ten years as an environmental researcher and activist in Indonesia. She is now a Fulbright Scholar at the University of Wisconsin/Madison in the Institute of Environmental Studies. Emmy is an active member of the Indonesian Environmental Forum and is currently on leave from WALHI, an Indonesian coalition of environmental groups.

References

Abdoellah, et. al., *Sustaining the Natural Resources of Kalimantan: An Interim Research Report* (draft). Mimeo.

Abdurrahman, 1984. *Hukum Adat Menurut Perundang Undangan Republik Indonesia.* [Customary Law According to the Legal System of the Republic of Indonesia]. Jakarta: Cendana Press.

Adams, D.M., K.C. Jackson, and R.W. Haynes. 1987. *Production, Consumption, and Prices of Softwood Products in North America: Regional Time Series Data, 1950–85.* U.S. Department of Agriculture, Forest Service, Pacific Northwest Forest and Range Experiment Station. Portland, OR.

Adams, D.M., and R.W. Haynes. 1990. Public policies, private resources, and the future of the Douglas-fir region forest economy. *Western Journal of Applied Forestry.* 5: 64–69.

Agee, J.K. and M.H. Huff. 1987. Fuel succession in a western hemlock/Douglas fir forest. *Canadian Journal of Forest Research.* 17: 697–704.

Aji, B., Karsadi, A.K. and Wahyuni, S. 1993 "Ya, Ya, Ya, Yamdena." *Tempo,* 18 September, 1993.

Anderson, H.M. and C. Gehrke. 1988. *National Forests: Policies for the Future. Volume 1: Water Quality and Timber Management.* The Wilderness Society, Washington, D.C.

Anderson, H.M. and J.T. Olson. 1991. *Federal Forests and the Economic Base of the Pacific Northwest.* The Wilderness Society, Washington, D.C.

Asian Development Bank (ADB), 1992. *Appraisal of the Biodiversity Conservation Project in Flores and Siberut in the Republic of Indonesia* (draft). Manila.

——. 1992a. *Indonesia: Private Sector Industrial Tree Plantations Program—Report of a Technical Assistance Consulting Team.* Manila.

Atkinson, W. 1990. Another view of New Forestry. *Forest Watch* 11(2): 12–15.

Aznam, S. 1992. "The toll of low wages", *Far Eastern Economic Review,* 2 April, 1992; 50.

Aznam, S. 1992a. "Help not wanted", *Far Eastern Economic Review,* 1 October, 1992; 18.

Aznam, S. 1992b. "Passport control: New immigration law can render citizens stateless", *Far Eastern Economic Review,* 26 March, 1992; 18.

Barber, C.V. 1992. Unpublished trip report on participation in the "Roundtable III" meeting on the Indonesian Forestry Action Programme, February 24–25, 1992, Yogjakarta, Indonesia.

——. 1990. *The Legal and Regulatory Framework for Forest Production in Indonesia.* Included as Appendix 1 in Zerner 1990.

——. 1989. *The State, The Environment, and Development: The Genesis and Transformation of Social Forestry Policy in New Order Indonesia*. Doctoral Dissertation, University of California, Berkeley.

Barber, C.V. and Churchill, G. 1987. *Land Policy in Irian Jaya: Issues and Strategies*. Jakarta; Government of Indonesia/United Nations Development Programme.

Bassett, P.M. and D.D. Oswald. 1983. *Timber Resource Statistics for Eastern Washington*. Resource Bulletin PNW-104. Pacific Northwest Research Station, Portland, OR.

Beuter, J.H. 1990. *Social and Economic Impacts of the Spotted Owl Conservation Strategy*. Technical Bulletin 9003. American Forest Resources Alliance, Washington, D.C.

Blahna, D.J. and S. Yonts-Shepard. 1989. Public involvement in resource planning: Toward bridging the gap between policy and implementation. *Society and Natural Resources*, 2: 209–227.

Bonnett, M. and K. Zimmerman. 1991. Politics and preservation: The Endangered Species Act and the northern spotted owl. *Ecology Law Quarterly*. 18: 105–171.

Booth, W. 1989. New thinking on old growth. *Science*, 244: 141–143.

Boulter, D. 1988. *Proposals for Medium and Long Term Planning for Forestry and Forest Sector Development in Indonesia* (draft). Jakarta; Paper prepared for FAO/UNDP project on "Assistance to Forest Sector Development Planning".

Boyd, R.G., and W.F. Hyde. 1989. *Forestry Sector Intervention: The Impacts of Public Regulation on Social Welfare*. Iowa State University Press, Ames, IA.

Bromley, D. 1989. Property relations and economic development: The other land reform. In *World Development*, Vol 17, No. 6, pp. 867–877.

Brookfield, H., et. al. 1990. Borneo and the Malay Peninsula, in B.L. Turner, et. al., eds., *The Earth as Transformed by Human Action*. Cambridge University Press.

Brown, G. and C.C. Harris. 1992. The U.S. Forest Service: Toward a new resource management paradigm? *Society and Natural Resources*, 5: 231–246.

Bruck, R.I. 1989. Forest decline syndromes in the southeastern United States. In: J.J. MacKenzie and M.T. El-Ashry, eds., *Air Pollution's Toll on Forests and Crops*, Yale University Press, New York. pp. 113–190.

Bundestag. 1990. *Protecting the Tropical Forests: A High Priority International Task*. 2nd report of the Enquet-Commission "Preventive Measures to Protect the Earth's Atmosphere." German Bundestag, Bonn.

Callister, D.J., 1992. *Illegal Tropical Timber Trade: Asia-Pacific*. Cambridge: TRAFFIC International.

Carroll, M.S. 1989. Taming the timberjack revisited. *Society and Natural Resources* 2: 91–106.

Cascade Holistic Environmental Consultants (CHEC), 1985. The politics of planning. *Forest Planning*, April 1985. CHEC, Eugene, OR.

Caufield, C. 1990. The ancient forest. *The New Yorker*, May 14, 1990: 46–84.

Clad, J. 1991. *Behind the Myth: Business, Money and Power in Southeast Asia*. London, Grafton Books.

Clary, D.A. 1986. *Timber and the Forest Service*. University Press of Kansas, Lawrence, KS.

Cleaver, K, M. Monasinghe, M. Dyson, N. Egli, A. Peuker, F. Wencelius. *Conservation of West and Central African Rainforests*. The World Bank, Washington, D.C.

Cohn, R. and T. Williams. 1993. Interior views. Interview with Interior Secretary Bruce Babbitt. *Audubon* 95(3): 78–84.

Colchester, M. 1990. *Shifting Cultivation: Rational Resource Use or Robber Economy?* Paper prepared for the Third World Network/APPEN Conference on "The Destruction of Asian Agriculture," Penang Malaysia, 10–13 January, 1990.

Colchester, M. and Lohmann, L. 1990. *The Tropical Forestry Action Plan: What Progress?* Penang, Malaysia, World Rainforest Movement.

Cort, C. 1991. *Voices From the Margin: Non-governmental Organization Participation in the Tropical Forestry Action Plan.* Washington, D.C., World Resources Institute.

Cubbage, F.W. 1991. Public regulation of private forestry. *Journal of Forestry* 89 (12): 31–35.

Cubbage, F.W., J. O'Laughlin, and C.S. Bullock III. 1993. *Forest Resource Policy.* John Wiley and Sons, New York.

Cubbage, F.W. and W.C. Siegal. 1985. The law regulating private forest practices. *Journal of Forestry* 83: 538–545.

de Beer, J. and McDermott, M. 1989. *The Economic Value of Non-timber Forest Products in Southeast Asia.* Amsterdam, Netherlands Committee for IUCN.

Departamen Kehutanan [Ministry of Forestry] 1991. *Social Forestry Development Project.* Report presented at a Coordinating Meeting of the Ministry of Forestry, 16 December, 1991. Jakarta: Mimeo.

____. 1986. *Sejarah Kehutanan Indonesia* [The History of Forestry in Indonesia]. Jakarta.

Dick 1991. *Forest Land Use, Forest Use Zonation, and Deforestation in Indonesia: A Summary and Interpretation of Existing Information.* WALHI, Jakarta.

Djamaluddin, S. 1991. *Pemanfaatan Hutan Yang Berkelanjutan* [Sustainable Forest Utilization]. Paper presented at Seminar on Sustainable Forest Utilization, 11 June 1991, Jakarta.

Douglas, J. 1985. *Organization for Production.* Paper presented at the Ninth World Forestry Congress, Mexico City, July 1985.

Dove, M. 1988. Introduction: Traditional Culture and Development in Contemporary Indonesia. In M. Dove, ed., *The Real and Imagined Role of Culture in Development: Case Studies from Indonesia.* Honolulu: University of Hawaii Press; 1–37.

____. 1985. The agroecological mythology of the Javanese and the political economy of Indonesia. *Indonesia* 39:1–36.

Dudley, N. 1992. *Forests in Trouble: A Review of the Status of Temperate Forests Worldwide.* Worldwide Fund for Nature, Gland, Switzerland.

Durning, A. 1992. *Guardians of the Land: Indigenous Peoples and the Health of the Earth.* Washington, D.C., Worldwatch Institute Paper 112.

Eagan, T. 1992. Space photos show forests in Pacific Northwest are in peril, scientists say. *New York Times,* June 11, 1992.

Economic and Social Commission for Asia and the Pacific (ESCAP), 1992. *State of the Environment in Asia and the Pacific 1990.* Bangkok: United Nations Economic and Social Commission for Asia and the Pacific, 15–16.

Ecotrust. 1992. Fiscal Year 1992 Annual Report. Ecotrust, Portland, Oregon.

Flora, D.F. 1990. Timber exports: Winners and losers. *Forest Watch* 10(11): 9–25.

Flora, D.F., A.L. Anderson, and W.J. McGinnis. 1991. *Pacific Rim Log Trade: Determinants and Trends.* Research Paper PNW-RP-432. Pacific Northwest Research Station, Portland, OR.

Flora, D.F., and W.J. McGinnis. 1989. Embargoes on and off: some effects of ending the export ban on federal logs and halting exports of state-owned logs. *Western Journal of Applied Forestry* 4(3): 77–79.

Food and Agriculture Organization of the United Nations (FAO), 1992. *Forest Products Annual Yearbook 1990*. FAO, Rome.

Forest Ecosystem Management Team (FEMAT), 1993. Forest Ecosystem Management: An Ecological, Economic, and Social Assessment. Report of the Forest Ecosystem Management Team. USDA, Washington, D.C.

Friedland, J. 1991. "Pulp and Paper: Aiming for a New Market. *Far Eastern Economic Review*. 18 April, 1991: 50.

Friends of the Earth. 1992. *Deserts of Trees: The Environmental and Social Impacts of Large-Scale Tropical Reforestation in Response to Global Climate Change*. London, Friends of The Earth, Ltd.

Gedney, D.R., P.M. Bassett, and M.A. Mei. 1989. *Timber Resource Statistics for All Forest Land, Except National Forests in Eastern Oregon*. USFS Resource Bulletin PNW-RB-164, Pacific Northwest Research Station, Portland, OR.

———. 1987. *Timber Resource Statistics for Non-Federal Forest Land in West-Central Oregon*. USFS Resource Bulletin PNW-RB-143, Pacific Northwest Research Station, Portland, OR.

———. 1986a. *Timber Resource Statistics for Non-Federal Forest Land in Northwest Oregon*. USFS Resource Bulletin PNW-RB-140, Pacific Northwest Research Station, Portland, OR.

———. 1986b. *Timber Resource Statistics for Non-Federal Forest Land in Southwest Oregon*. USFS Resource Bulletin PNW-RB-138, Pacific Northwest Research Station, Portland, OR.

Gillis, M. 1988. Indonesia: Public Policies, Resource Management, and the Tropical Forest. In R. Repetto and M. Gillis, eds., *Public Policies and the Misuse of Forest Resources*. Cambridge University Press.

GOI (Government of Indonesia) 1991. *Indonesia Forestry Action Programme*. Jakarta.

———. 1991a. *Industrial Forestry Plantation and Forest Rehabilitation*. Jakarta, Ministry of Forestry.

———. 1991b. *Biodiversity Action Plan for Indonesia* (final draft). Jakarta.

———. 1990. *Summary: Situation and Outlook of the Forestry Sector in Indonesia*. Seminar Technical Report, Forestry Studies Project, 8 December, 1990. Jakarta, Department of Forestry. [Produced in both English and Bahasa Indonesia.]

———. 1974–1990. *Himpunan Peraturan Perundangan di Bidang Kehutanan Indonesia, Jilid I–VIII* [Compilation of Laws and Regulations in the Indonesian Forestry Sector, Vols. I–VIII]. Jakarta, Ministry of Forestry.

GOI/FAO [Government of Indonesia/United Nations Food and Agriculture Organization] 1990. *Situation and Outlook of the Forestry Sector in Indonesia*. Jakarta. [In four volumes.]

Gordon, J.C., J.F. Franklin, K.N. Johnson, and J.W. Thomas. *1991. Alternatives for the Management of Late Successional Forests of the Pacific Northwest: Report of the Scientific Panel on Late Successional Forest Ecosystems*. U.S. House of Representatives, Committee on Agriculture, Washington.

Gorte, R.W. 1989. *National Forest Receipts: Sources and Dispositions*. Report No. 89-284. U.S. Library of Congress, Congressional Research Service, Washington, D.C.

Gottlieb, A.M. 1989. *The Wise Use Agenda: The Citizen's Policy Guide to Environmental Resource Issues*. Merril Press, Bellevue, WA.

Gray, J.A. and S. Hadi. 1989. *Forest Concessions in Indonesia: Institutional Aspects*. Jakarta, Government of Indonesia/FAO.

Greene, S. 1988. Research Natural Areas and Protecting Old-growth Forests on Public Lands in Western Oregon and Washington. *Natural Areas Journal*, 8: 25–30.

Gregg, N.T. 1991. Will "New Forestry" Save Old Forests? *American Forests*, 97: 49–53.

Gunawan, G. 1991. *Sistem Silvikultur Dalam Pengusahaan Hutan Alam Produksi Indonesia.* [The Silvicultural System in the Exploitation of Natural Production Forests in Indonesia.] Jakarta, WALHI.

Guppy, N. 1984. Tropical deforestation: A global view. *Foreign Affairs* 62: 928–965.

Haeruman, H. 1992. *Masalah Sosial dalam Pembangunan Kehutanan* [Social Problems in Forestry Development]. *Andal* No. 12. Jakarta.

Hansen, A.J., T.A. Spies, F.J. Swanson, and J.L. Ohmann. 1991. Conserving biodiversity in managed forests. *BioScience*, 41: 382–392.

Hansen, G. and Mahoney, T. 1978. Rural Organizations and Development in Indonesia. In Inayatullah, ed., *Rural Organizations and Rural Development*. Kuala Lumpur; Asia and the Pacific Development Administration Center.

Haynes, R.W. 1992. Owls, jobs, and old growth. *Forest Watch* 12(10): 15–17.

———. 1986. *Inventory and Value of Old Growth in the Douglas Fir Region.* Research Note PNW 437. Pacific Northwest Research Station, Portland, OR.

Honadle, G. 1993. Institutional constraints on sustainable resource use: Lessons from the tropics showing that resource over exploitation is not just an attitude problem and conservation education is not enough. In: G.H. Aplet, N. Johnson, J.T. Olson, and V.A. Sample, eds., *Defining Sustainable Forestry*. Island Press, Washington, D.C.

IIASA. 1990. The price of pollution. *Options,* International Institute for Applied Systems Analysis, Vienna, Austria.

IIED/GOI [International Institute for Environment and Development/Government of Indonesia] 1985. *Forest Policies in Indonesia.* Jakarta.

Indonesian Business Weekly. 1993. "A Public Concern." September 3, 1993.

Indonesian Observer. 1993. "Real Nomadic Farmers Do Not Destroy Forests." 3 February, 1993. [Reporting on an address by Professor Mubyarto of Gadjah Mada University at a government workshop on managing shifting cultivation. Mubyarto is currently a senior official at BAPPENAS—the National Development Planning Agency.]

Irwin, L.L., and T.B. Wigley. 1992. Conservation of Endangered Species. *Journal of Forestry* 90: 27–30.

Jackson, K.D. 1978. The Political Implications of Structure and Culture in Indonesia. In Jackson, K.D. and Pye, L., eds. *Political Power and Communications in Indonesia.* Berkeley, University of California Press.

Jakarta Post. 1993. "Operations against illegal logging." April 5, 1993.

———. 1993a. "Plywood firms complain of log shortages." September 3, 1993.

———. 1993b. "10,000 forest squatter families to be resettled." 9 September, 1993.

———. 1993c. "Logging activities in Yamdena to restart despite stay order." 18 January, 1993.

———. 1993d. "Yamdena logging row to be settled soon." 4 February, 1993.

———. 1993e. "Government to allow resumption of logging on Yamdena island." 11 September, 1993.

Johnson, A.H., and T.G. Siccama. 1989. Decline of red spruce in the high elevation forests of the northeastern United States. In: J.J. MacKenzie and M.T. El-Ashry, eds. *Air Pollution's Toll on Forests and Crops.* Yale University Press, New York. pp. 191–234.

Johnson, N. and B. Cabarle. 1993. *Surviving the Cut: Natural Forest Management in the Humid Tropics*. World Resources Institute, Washington, D.C.

Kerr, A. 1990. New (age) perspectives: glossy dogma to hide old habits. *Forest Watch* 11(4): 22–26.

KLH [Indonesian Ministry of State for Population and Environment] 1992. *Indonesia Country Study on Biological Diversity*. Jakarta.

Knize, P. 1991. The mismanagement of the National Forests. *Atlantic* 268: 21–29.

Lee, R.G., P Sommers, H. Birss, C. Nasser, and J. Zientek. 1991. *Social Impacts of Alternative Timber Harvest Reductions on Federal Lands in O and C Counties. Final Report for the Association of O and C Counties*. Northwest Policy Center, University of Washington. Seattle, WA.

Levin, J. 1992. Russian forest laws—scant protection during troubled times. Manuscript submitted for publication in Ecology Law Quarterly.

Levy, D. 1977. Judicial Authority and Rechstaat in Indonesia. In R. Vuylsteke, ed. 1977. *Law and Society: Culture Learning Through Law*. Honolulu; East-West Center.

Little, C.E. 1992. Report from Lucy's Woods. American Forests, 98(2): 25–27, 68–69.

Long, J. 1991. Cheating on sales of timber costing millions every year. *The Oregonian* (Portland), November 17, 1991.

Lyden, F.J., B.W. Twight, and E.T. Tuchmann. 1990. Citizen participation in long-range planning: The RPA experience. *Natural Resources Journal*. 30: 123–138.

MacCleery, D.W. 1991. Condition and trends of U.S. Forests: a brief overview. USDA Forest Service, Timber Management Staff. Washington, D.C.

MacKenzie, J.J., and M.T. El-Ashry. 1989. Tree and crop injury: A summary of the evidence. In: J.J. MacKenzie and M.T. El-Ashry, eds., *Air Pollution's Toll on Forests and Crops*. Yale University Press, New York, pp. 1–21.

MacLean, C.D., P.M. Bassett, and G. Yeary. 1992. *Timber Resource Statistics for Western Washington*. USFS Resource Bulletin PNW-RB-191. Pacific Northwest Research Station, Portland, OR.

Manning, C. 1971. The timber boom. In *The Bulletin of Indonesian Economic Studies*, Vol. 7, No. 3. (Cited in Robison 1978.)

Marks, P, J.D. Allan, C. Canham, K. Van Cleve, A. Covich, and F. James. 1993. Scientific Peer Review of the Ecological Aspects of Forest Ecosystem Management: An Ecological, Economic, and Social Assessment. Report by an *ad-hoc* committee of The Ecological Society of America and The American Institute of Biological Sciences. The Ecological Society of America, Washington, D.C.

Miller, P.R. 1989. Concept of forest decline in the western United States. In: J.J. MacKenzie and M.T. El-Ashry, eds., *Air Pollution's Toll on Forests and Crops*. Yale University Press, New York, pp. 75–112.

Moniaga, S. 1991. *Towards Community-Based Forestry and Recognition of Adat Property Rights in the Outer Islands of Indonesia: A Legal and Policy Analysis*. Paper presented at the Workshop on Legal Issues in Social Forestry, Bali, 4–6 November 1991.

Morrison, P.H. 1988. *Old Growth in the Pacific Northwest: A Status Report*. The Wilderness Society, Washington, D.C.

Myers, N. 1989. *Deforestation Rates in Tropical Forests and Their Climatic Implications*. London, Friends of the Earth.

Neraca, April 6, 1993. [Jakarta newspaper]. *Menhut Menjamin Eksistensi Hak Adat di Hutan*.

[Minister of Forestry Guarantees the Existence of Customary Rights in the Forest.]

Newsletter of the New England Environmental Network (NEEN), 1992. Eastern Old Growth Surveyed. *Environmental News: The Newsletter of the New England Environmental Network*. Vol. 9 (4). Tufts University, Medford, MA.

Ngo, M. 1991. *Ambiguity in Property Rights: Lessons from the Kayan of Kalimantan*. Paper presented at the conference on "Interactions of People and Forests in Kalimantan", New York Botanical Garden, 21–23 June, 1991.

NLMP. 1993. Contributions from environmental groups and the timber and paper industry to all congressional candidates: 1/1/85–6/30/92. Printouts from database maintained by National Library on Money and Politics, based on Federal Election Commission records. National Library on Money and Politics, Washington, D.C.

Norse, E.A. 1990. *Ancient Forests of the Pacific Northwest*. Island Press, Washington, D.C.

Norse, E.A., K.L. Rosenbaum, D.S. Wilcove, B.A. Wilcox, W.H. Romme, D. Johnston, and M.L. Stout. 1986. Conserving Biological Diversity in our National Forests. The Wilderness Society, Washington, D.C.

Northwest Policy Center. 1992. Responding to the Northwest's workforce challenge. *The Changing Northwest*, 4(3): 1–6. Newsletter of the Northwest Policy Center, Seattle, WA.

NRC (National Research Council). 1993. *Sustainable Agriculture and the Environment in the Humid Tropics* Washington, D.C., National Academy Press.

Nugroho, T. 1991. *Studi Sekunder Konsep dan Implementasi Pembangunan Hutan Tanaman Industri di Indonesia* [Desk Study on the Concept and Implementation of Industrial Timber Plantation Development in Indonesia]. Jakarta, WALHI.

ODA, 1992. *Sustainable Forest Management in KPHPs*. UK/Indonesia Tropical Forest Management Project Discussion Paper. Jakarta.

Olson, J.T. 1988. *National Forests: Policies for the Future. Volume 4: Pacific Northwest Lumber and Wood Products: An Industry in Transition*. The Wilderness Society, Washington, D.C.

OMB. 1992. *Budget of the United States Government, Fiscal Year 1993*. Executive Office of the President, Office of Management and Budget, Washington, D.C.

Oregon Department of Forestry. 1991. *Forest Practice Rules*. Published October 29, 1991. Forest Practices Section, Oregon Department of Forestry, Salem, OR.

Oregonian. 1993a. Log export tax breaks face ax. *The Oregonian* (Portland), May 6, 1993.

———. 1993b. Forest plan faces another challenge. *The Oregonian* (Portland), October 27, 1993.

Ostergaard, L., Traditional Swidden Cultivators and Forces of Deforestation in Sumatra: The Significance of Local Land Tenure Systems. Paper presented at the Second Asia-Pacific Consultative Meeting on Biodiversity Conservation, 2–6 February, 1993, Bangkok, Thailand.

OTA. 1992. *Forest Service Planning: Accommodating Uses, Producing Outputs, and Sustaining Ecosystems*. Office of Technology Assessment, Washington, D.C.

———. 1990. *Forest Service Planning: Setting Strategic Direction under RPA*. Office of Technology Assessment, Washington, D.C.

O'Toole, R. 1993. Recalculating the 1992 TSPIRS. *Forest Watch*, 14(6).

———. 1988. *Reforming the Forest Service*. Island Press, Washington, D.C.

Peluso, N. 1988. *Rich Forests, Poor People, and Development: Forest Access Control and Resistance in*

Java. Doctoral dissertation. Ithaca, N.Y., Cornell University.

——. 1986. *Rattan Industries in East Kalimantan, Indonesia*. Paper commissioned by United Nations Food and Agriculture Organization, Forestry Department. Rome.

Perry, D.A. 1988. Landscape pattern and forest pests. *Northwest Environmental Journal*, 4: 213–228.

Perry, G., and A. Perry. 1983. *Guide to Natural Areas of Oregon and Washington*. Sierra Club Books, San Francisco.

Poffenberger, Ed. 1990. *Keepers of the Forest: Land Management Alternatives in Southeast Asia*. West Hartford, Kumarian Press.

Postel, S. and J. C. Ryan. 1991. Reforming forestry. In: L. Brown, ed., *State of the World 1991*. W. W. Norton and Company, New York. pp. 74–92.

Potter, L. 1991. Forest Degradation, Deforestation and Reforestation in Kalimantan: Towards a Sustainable Land Use? Paper presented at the conference on "Interactions of People and Forests in Kalimantan", New York Botanical Garden, 21–23 June, 1991.

Pramono, A.H. 1991. *A Brief Review on Forest Land Use and Deforestation in Indonesia*. WALHI. Jakarta.

Raikes, P. 1988. *Modernizing Hunger*. London: Catholic Institute for International Relations, v.

Ramakrishna, K. and G.M. Woodwell. *World Forests for the Future: Their Use and Conservation*. Yale University Press, New Haven, CT.

Rasmussen, M, D. Olson, and W. Maki. 1991. Social and economic impacts in Washington, Oregon, and California associated with implementing the proposed critical habitat designation. In: *Comments on the Designation of Critical Habitat for the Northern Spotted Owl on National Forests*, American Forest Resource Council, Washington.

Reid, W.V. and Miller, K.R. 1989. *Keeping Options Alive: The Scientific Basis for Conserving Biodiversity*. Washington, D.C., World Resources Institute.

Repetto, R. 1988. Subsidized timber sales for national forest lands in the United States. In: R. Repetto and M. Gillis, eds., *Public Policies and the Misuse of Forest Resources*. Cambridge University Press, New York. pp. 353–383.

Repetto, R., R.C. Dower, R. Jenkins and J. Geoghehan. 1992. *Green Fees: How a Tax Shift Can Work for the Environment and the Economy*. World Resources Insitute, Washington, D.C.

Repetto, R. and M. Gillis. 1988. *Public Policies and the Misuse of Forest Resources*. Cambridge University Press, New York.

Repetto, R., W. Magrath, M. Wells, C. Beer, and F. Rossini. 1989. *Wasting Assets: Natural Resources in the National Income Accounts*. World Resources Institute, Washington, D.C.

RePPProT [Regional Physical Planning Programme for Transmigration] 1990. *The Land Resources of Indonesia: A National Overview*. Overseas Development Administration (UK) and Department of Transmigration (Indonesia), Jakarta.

Rice, R.E. 1989. *National Forests—Policies for the Future: Volume 5: The Uncounted Costs of Logging*. The Wilderness Society, Washington, D.C.

Rivlin, A.M. 1993. Values, institutions, and sustainable forestry. In: G.H. Aplet, N. Johnson, J. Olson, and V.A. Sample, eds., *Defining Sustainable Forestry*. Island Press, Washington, D.C.

Roberts, E.F. 1974. A basic introduction to land use control and doctrine. In: *Proceedings of the Conference on Rural Land-Use Policy in the Northeast*. Cornell University, Ithaca, NY.

Robertson, F.D. 1992. Ecosystem management of the national forests and grasslands. Memo to Regional Foresters and Station Directors, USDA Forest Service, Washington, D.C.: June 4, 1992.

Romm, J. 1993. Sustainable forestry and sustainable forests. In: G.H. Aplet, N. Johnson, J. Olson, and V.A. Sample, eds., *Defining Sustainable Forestry*. Island Press, Washington, D.C.

Salazar, D.J. and F.W. Cubbage. 1990. Regulating forestry in the West and South. *Journal of Forestry* 88: 14–19.

Sample, A. 1984. *Below-Cost Timber Sales on the National Forests*. The Wilderness Society, Washington, D.C.

Sample, A.V. 1992. Resource planning and budgeting for National Forest management. *Public Administration Review*. 52: 339–346.

———. 1990. *The Impact of the Federal Budget Process on National Forest Planning*. Greenwood Press, New York.

———. 1989. What's really driving National Forest management? *American Forests*, 95(1): 58–69.

Sample, A.V. and D. LeMaster. 1992. *Assessing the Employment Impacts of the Proposed Measures to Protect the Spotted Owl*. American Forestry Association, Washington, D.C.

Schneider, K. 1993. U.S. would end cutting of trees in many forests. *New York Times*, April 30, 1993.

Schwarz, A. 1992a. "Timber is the Test: Forestry Controls Dampen Export Earnings". *Far Eastern Economic Review*, 23 July, 1992: 36.

Schwarz, A. and J. Friedland 1992b. "Green Fingers: Indonesia's Prajogo proves that money grows on trees." *Far Eastern Economic Review*, 12 March, 1992: 42.

Schwarz, A. 1992c. "Trade for Trees: Tariff reform will help save the forests". *Far Eastern Economic Review*. 4 June, 1992: 60.

Scott, J. 1985. *Weapons of the Weak: Everyday Forms of Peasant Resistance*. New Haven, Conn., Yale University Press.

Sedjo, R. 1988. *Native Forests, Secondary Species, Plantation Forests and the Sustainability of Indonesia's Forest Industry*. Jakarta; Paper prepared for FAO/UNDP project on "Assistance to Forest Sector Development Planning."

———. 1987. *Incentives and Distortions in Indonesian Forest Policy*. Unpublished report prepared for World Bank. Jakarta.

Sedjo, R.A., A.C. Wiseman, and K.S. Lyon. 1992. Exploiting National Returns to Log Exports. *Journal of Forestry* 90: 35–39.

Sessions, J., K.N. Johnson, J. Beuter, Brian Greber, and G. Lettmann. 1990. *Timber for Oregon's Tomorrow: The 1989 Update*. Oregon State University, Corvallis, OR.

Seymour, F. and Rutherford, D. 1990. *Contractual Agreements in Asian Social Forestry Programs*. Paper prepared for the First Annual Meeting of the International Association for the Study of Common Property, 27–30 September, 1990, Duke University, Durham, North Carolina.

Seymour, F., et. al. 1993. *Summary of Findings and Recommendations of the Environmental Assessment of the Indonesia Natural Resources Management Project (Final Draft)*. Washington, D.C.: Biodiversity Support Program.

Shannon, M.A. 1990. *Public Participation in the RPA Process*. OTA background paper. Office of Technology Assessment, Washington, D.C.

Sharma, N.P. 1992. *Managing the World's Forests*. Dubuque, Iowa: Kendall/Hunt, 1.

Shin, Y.H. 1989. *Demystifying the Capitalist State: Political Patronage, Bureaucratic Interests, and Capitalists-in-Formation in Soeharto's Indonesia*. Doctoral Dissertation, Yale University.

Showalter, T.D. and J.E. Means. Pest response to simplification of forest landscapes. *Northwest Environmental Journal* 4: 342–343.

Soeharto, 1993. Speech by the President of the Republic of Indonesia His Excellency Soeharto at the Opening of the Global Forest Conference, Jakarta, 17 February, 1993.

Sommers, P. 1988. State of the Northwest. In: P. Sommers, W.E. Whitelaw, E. Niemi, and D.S. Harrison, eds., *The Once and Future Northwest*. Northwest Policy Center, Seattle, WA.

Sonner, S. 1993. Federal report sees costly timber theft, fraud. *The Oregonian* (Portland), May 4, 1993.

St. Clair, J. Cutting it down the middle: Clinton opts for experimental strategy in Northwest forests. *Forest Watch*, 14 (1): 4–12.

Sudiyat, I., 1981. *Hukum Adat*. [Customary Law]. Yogyakarta: Liberty.

Suharyanto, H. 1993. "Foresters Fall Short of Targets." *Indonesian Business Weekly*, July 16, 1993.

Syukur, H. 1993. "Dari Hutan ke Pengadilan" [From the Forest to Court], *Tempo*, 18 September, 1993: 82.

Thang, H. 1989. *Forest Conservation and Management Practices in Malaysia*. Paper presented at workshop on "Realistic Strategies for Tropical Forests", IUCN General Assembly, Perth, Australia, 28 November–5 December 1990. (Cited in Potter 1991.)

Thomas, J.W., M.G. Raphael, R.G. Anthony, E.D. Forsman, A.G. Gunderson, R.S. Holthausen, B.G. Marcot, G.H. Reeves, J.R. Sedell, D.M. Solis. 1993. *Viability Assessments and Management Considerations for Species Associated with Late-Successional and Old-Growth Forest of the Pacific Northwest*. Report of USDA Forest Service Scientific Analysis Team to U.S. District Court Judge William L. Dwyer. USDA Forest Service Research, Washington, D.C.

Thomas, J.W., E.D. Forsman, J.B. Lint, E.C. Meslow, B.R. Noon, and J. Verner. 1990. *A Conservation Strategy for the Northern Spotted Owl: Report of the Interagency Scientific Committee to Address the Conservation of the Northern Spotted Owl*. USDA Forest Service, Portland, Oregon.

Tjitradjaja, I., 1991. *Differential Access to Resources and Conflict Resolution in a Forest Concession in Irian Jaya*. Paper presented at the workshop on "Legal Issues in Social Forestry," Bali, Indonesia, November 4–6, 1991.

Ulrich, A.H. 1990. *U.S. Timber Production, Trade, Consumption and Price Statistics 1960–1988*. Miscellaneous Publication No. 1486, USDA, Washington, D.C.

UN-ECE/FAO. 1992. *The Forest Resources of the Temperate Zones: Main Findings of the UN-ECE/FAO 1990 Forest Resource Assessment*. United Nations, New York.

United States Department of Agriculture (USDA), 1993a. 1992 Annual Report: Timber Sale Program Information Reporting System, Washington, D.C.

———. 1993b. Draft Supplemental Environmental Impact Statement on Management of Habitat for Late Successional and Old-Growth Related Species within the Range of the Northern Spotted Owl. USDA Forest Service, Washington, DC.

———. 1992. *Report of the Forest Service: Fiscal Year 1991*. USDA Forest Service, Washington, D.C.

———. 1989. *RPA Assessment of the Forest and Rangeland Situation in the United States, 1989*. Forest Service Report No. 26. USDA Forest Service, Washington, D.C.

———. 1987. *Rise to the Future: The Fisheries Program of the USDA Forest Service*. U.S. Forest Service, Washington, D.C.

U.S. Department of Commerce. 1992. *Statistical Abstract of the United States 1992*. U.S. Department of Commerce Bureau of the Census, Washington, D.C.

———. 1991. *Statistical Abstract of the United States 1991*. U.S. Department of Commerce Bureau of the Census, Washington, D.C.

U.S. Department of Interior Fish and Wildlife Service (USFWS), 1992. *Critical Habitat for the Northern Spotted Owl*. U.S. Department of Interior Fish and Wildlife Service, Washington, D.C.

———. 1990. *Status Review for the Northern Spotted Owl*. U.S. Department of Interior Fish and Wildlife Service, Washington, D.C.

———. 1988. *1985 Survey of Fishing, Hunting, and Wildlife Associated Recreation*. U.S. Department of Interior Fish and Wildlife Service, Washington, D.C.

Vatakiotis, M. 1989. "Order in Court", *Far Eastern Economic Review*, 15 June 1989: 28.

Waddell, K.L., D.D. Oswald, and D.S. Powell. 1989. *Forest Statistics of the United States*. Resource Bulletin PNW-RB-168. Pacific Northwest Research Station, Portland, OR.

WALHI, (Indonesian Forum for the Environment) 1993. *Victims of Development, Environesia*, Vol. 7, No. 1 (1993).

———. 1993a. *Violated Trust: Disregard for the Forests and Forest Laws of Indonesia*. Jakarta.

———. 1992. *Peran HPH dalam Pembangunan Ekonomi Regional Kalimantan Timur* [The Role of Timber Concessions in the Regional Economic Development of East Kalimantan]. Jakarta.

———. 1991. *Sustainability and Economic Rent in the Indonesia Forestry Sector*. Jakarta.

WALHI/LBH (Indonesian Forum for the Environment/Indonesian Legal Aid Institute) 1992. *Mistaking Plantations for the Forest: Indonesia's Pulp and Paper Industry, Communities, and Environment*. Jakarta.

Walth, B. 1992. Timber industry bankrolled recall bid. *Eugene Register-Guard* (OR),October 6, 1992.

Warta Ekonomi [Economic News] 1990. *Hutan, Pengusaha, dan Nasibnya* [Forests, Businessmen, and their Fate], No. 24, 23 April, 1990.

Washington State Employment Security. 1993. *Washington Labor Market Highlights*, 17(2): 13.

———. 1992a. *Employment and Payrolls in Washington State by County and Industry: 1990 Annual Averages*. Washington State Employment Security Office, Olympia, WA.

———. 1992b. *Washington Labor Market Highlights* 16: 1–16.

Washington State Office of Financial Management. 1992. *Washington State 1991 Data Book*. Washington Office of Financial Management, Olympia, WA.

Weinstock, J. 1989. *Study on Shifting Cultivation in Indonesia* (draft). Jakarta, Ministry of Forestry.

Wells, D.R. 1971. *Survival of the Malaysian Bird Fauna*. In *Malayan Nature Journal*, Vol. 24, 248-256. (Cited in Whitmore 1984.)

Weyerhauser. *Weyerhauser 1992 Annual Report*. Weyerhauser Company, Seattle, WA.

Wiersum, K.F. 1987. *International Experience in Social Forestry and Implications for Research Support*. Paper presented at the Conference on Planning and Implementation of Social Forestry Programs in Indonesia", Gadjah Mada University, Yogyakarta, 1–3 December, 1987.

Wilcove, D. 1988. *National Forests: Policies for the Future. Volume 2: Protecting Biological Diversity*. The Wilderness Society, Washington, D.C.

Wilderness Society. 1988. *End of the Ancient Forests: Special Report on National Forest Plans in the Pacific Northwest*. The Wilderness Society, Washington, D.C.

Winterbottom, R. 1990. *Taking Stock: The Tropical Forestry Action Plan After Five Years*. Washington, D.C., World Resources Institute.

World Bank 1993. *Indonesia: Sustaining Development*. Washington, D.C.

——. 1991. *Malaysia Forestry Subsector Study* (draft). Washington, D.C.

——. 1991a. *Indonesia: Developing Private Enterprise*. Washington, D.C.

——. 1991b. *The Forest Sector—A World Bank Policy Paper*. Washington, D.C.

——. 1990. *Indonesia Poverty Assessment and Strategy Report*. Washington, D.C.

——. 1989. *Indonesia—Forest Land and Water: Issues in Sustainable Development*. Washington, D.C.

——. 1988. *Indonesia: Adjustment, Growth and Sustainable Development*. Washington, D.C.

World Resources Institute (WRI). 1992. *World Resources 1992–93: A Guide to the Global Environment*. Oxford University Press, New York.

Wyant, W.K. 1982. *Westward in Eden. The Public Lands and The Conservation Movement*. University of California Press, Berkeley, CA.

YLBHI [Indonesian Legal Aid Foundation], *The Torching of the People's Homes and the Destruction of Their Fields in Subdistrict Pulau Panggung, Lampung Selatan, Sumatra, Indonesia*. Jakarta: Mimeo.

Yoho, J.G. 1985. Continuing Investments in Forestry: Private Investment Strategies. In: *Investments in Forestry: Resources, Land Use, and Public Policy*. R.A. Sedjo, ed. Westview Press, Boulder, CO. pp. 151–166.

Zerner, C. 1990. *Legal Options for the Indonesian Forestry Sector*. Goverment of Indonesia/ United Nations Food and Agriculture Organization. Jakarta.